About the Author

Kate Orson is a Hand in Hand Parenting instructor and writer. She was born in the UK and now lives in Basel, Switzerland with her husband, the author Toni Davidson, and their daughter. Kate has an MPhil in Creative Writing from the University of Glasgow. Kate teaches parenting workshops and gives consultations online and in the UK and Switzerland. She has written for UK parenting magazines the *Green Parent*, *Juno* and *Smallish*.

Tears Heal

How to listen to our children

KATE ORSON

piatkus

PIATKUS

First published in Great Britain in 2016 by Piatkus

1 3 5 7 9 10 8 6 4 2

A CIP catalogue record for this book
is available from the British Library.

ISBN 978-0-349-41010-4

Typeset in Stone Serif and Futura by M Rules
Printed and bound in Great Britain by
Clays Ltd, St Ives plc

Papers used by Piatkus are from well-managed forests
and other responsible sources.

MIX
Paper from
responsible sources
FSC® C104740

Piatkus
An imprint of
Little, Brown Book Group
Carmelite House
50 Victoria Embankment
London EC4Y 0DZ

An Hachette UK Company
www.hachette.co.uk

www.improvementzone.co.uk

For Toni and Ruby, and for all our children.
In memory of my grandmother, Olga Orson.

Contents

Acknowledgements

Thank you to Patty Wipfler, Julianne Idleman and everyone at Hand in Hand Parenting for all their support and encouragement. Without you this book wouldn't have existed.

Thanks to the first readers of the introduction, Jodie Eastwood, Lucy Forward and Dina Sabry Fivaz, who were there to encourage me in the early stages.

Thanks also to all the members of the Thin Raft writer's group for all their helpful feedback and support. Thanks to my friends Bronwyn Nugent, Sara Whittleton and Jessica Jarret Cade for great conversations about parenting and for always believing in this book.

Thanks to John Munro for being there to calm my nerves during my search for an agent.

A big thank you to all of my listening partners, Otilia Mantelers, Ceci Hyoun, Maya Coleman, Stephanie Parker and Sarah Charlton, who were there every step of the way to help me repair and heal the dents in my confidence and to listen to my worries and anxieties.

Special thanks to my wonderful husband and brilliant dad, Toni Davidson, for always being there to cook hot meals and sort out the practical side of life when my mind was elsewhere.

Extra big thanks to my daughter, Ruby, for allowing me all this time to write! Writing is not easy, but having you in my life has made this book possible. Lots of love to you all.

And finally thanks to my agent, Clare Hulton, and my editor at Piatkus, Anne Lawrance, for seeing this book's potential – thank you for your support in making it a reality.

Foreword

Many parents of young children find themselves in a difficult spot. The 'command and control' parenting approach, once so common, doesn't seem to fit our families well in current times. Parents used to tell their children what to do and how to feel. There were punishments for misbehaviour, harsh words and judgement. Children were expected to do exactly what their parents wanted, when they wanted it. But today's parents have tried dominating and intimidating their children, and they don't like it. They don't want to spank. They don't want to yell. And they get tired of lecturing and bribing their children in their efforts to get through the day.

In addition, many of today's parents have noticed that spanking, yelling, lecturing and even systems of positive rewards fail to sway a young mind for long. The same old difficulties boomerang back into play, making parenting ever more frustrating. Moreover, modern societies have rightly begun to frown on hitting children when their behaviour is not up to scratch. But how, then, can a parent stop their child from grabbing toys away from other children? What in the world will keep their little ones from fighting daily over who gets the yellow cup?

Tears Heal is a warm and personal introduction to a new way of parenting – Hand in Hand Parenting – that has listening at its core. Parents looking for a parenting approach that is practical, effective and generous in its outlook on children will find it here.

Kate Orson takes us through her own journey with Hand in

Hand Parenting. She gives us windows into her thinking and experience as she describes a new way to interact with our children. She shows how and why tears heal. The insight she returns to again and again is that your child's upsets are an opportunity. Listening while your child cries – after you've checked her health and safety, of course – can relieve her of the tension that clouds her behaviour and makes your day difficult. As you listen and your child's tears flow, you help her heal today's upsets, and even those she's held for months or years. And as your child heals, her judgement will improve.

You will gently be shown what a transformative difference listening can make in your own life, as well. You'll learn how to set up a listening partnership with another parent, so you can shed the everyday tensions that can mount as you throw your whole heart, and so much of your time and energy, into loving your child. Simple exercises at the end of each chapter will prompt you to explore your own attitudes and experience, which underlie your responses to your child's struggles and behaviour.

We parents learn well from one another's stories. Kate's transparency about her own evolution as a mother is a form of generosity, I think. Most of us feel alone with our parenting challenges. Sometimes we even feel ashamed about what we haven't yet figured out. When Kate uses the challenges she has faced to illustrate important concepts, it's easier to remember that struggles are par for the course in parenting. Kate takes the reader by the hand. Her openness says, 'I understand. Parenting is hard work. None of us get it right all the time!'

In *Tears Heal*, you'll find research to intrigue you, and parent stories to illuminate central ideas. There are chapters that will finally explain why your child cries on and on about a Lego piece that has fallen behind the radiator, when he's got ten others just like it, and why he asks for orange juice, then rejects it, then cries when you put it back in the fridge. The tools she suggests are ones I've worked with for over forty years. They are simple, and they work. They help you get through your days with a young child without punishment or intimidation. They will lead you towards more rewarding times as a parent, because, at last, you will be working *with* your child's instinct to heal from emotional hurt. And as you do, you'll believe more firmly in his goodness, no matter how he's behaving at the moment.

Hand in Hand Parenting is a new parenting approach for a new age. We and our children are challenged to make sense of a torrent of information each day. We live in diverse communities, and the issues before us as a human community are complex indeed. If we hope to raise children who can thrive in today's world and contribute to their communities, we must adopt parenting practices that build their confidence and support their inborn intelligence from the start.

As Kate unfolds the Hand in Hand Parenting ideas, you'll see that the emphasis on allowing our tears to heal our heartbreak will do just that. Listening, parent to parent and parent to child, is the compassionate response to a loved one's grief. It's also the response that frees us – parents and children alike – to connect, cooperate and enjoy one another.

I hope you are encouraged by this new way of responding to children. I hope you are intrigued by the possibilities of building good support for the challenging work of parenting. You deserve good support as a mother or father. After all, what more important work will you do?

You want to give your best to your child, and the insights and practices Kate provides in *Tears Heal* are just what you've been looking for. You have in your hand tools for these times: tools to help relieve the stresses of parenting. Tools to deliver your love and your confidence straight to your crying child's heart.

Patty Wipfler, Founder and Program Director, Hand in Hand Parenting and author of *Listen: Five Simple Tools to Meet Your Everyday Parenting Challenges*

Tears, the Paradigm Shift

•

'But a mermaid has no tears, and therefore
she suffers so much more.'

Hans Christian Andersen,
The Little Mermaid

Tears heal. We all know the feeling of having a good cry,
especially in the presence of someone we love. Shakespeare
wrote that 'to weep is to make less the depth of grief', and now
scientific research supports what writers and thinkers have
intuitively sensed for years, that crying makes us feel happier
and healthier, and that it is part of our body and mind's natural
inbuilt process for recovering from stress and upset.

As parents of infants and toddlers, however, we find that tears
are one of the most challenging aspects of our role. We tend to
judge the success of our parenting by how much our children
cry. We feel like wonderful parents when our babies are smiley
and at ease, but we feel terrible when they cry for what seems to
be no reason and we just can't get them to stop.

William Frey, a biochemist, conducted a pioneering inves-
tigation of the chemical composition of tears. He found that
those shed for emotional reasons contained cortisol – the stress
hormone – whereas those induced by raw onions contained only
saline solution.[1] This suggests that when we cry for emotional
reasons we are literally releasing stress from our bodies and that

crying is an essential part of the recovery process from stress and trauma.

Seen from this perspective, having a colicky baby or a tantrumming toddler is not necessarily a direct reflection of how we are parenting but more to do with the experiences our child has had, or is going through – experiences that are often completely out of our control. Life is full of events and changes that can bring stress to our families. As parents, we are all trying our best, and just because your child is having an emotional upset it doesn't mean that you aren't doing a good job.

In this book I'll reveal the secret healing potential of our children's tears and introduce a paradigm shift in our thinking about crying: that when we move away from controlling emotions towards listening instead, family life is transformed.

This book also introduces a new way of looking at behaviour: that our children are naturally good, loving and cooperative and that they want to get on well with us, their siblings and their friends. I'll reveal why they behave in challenging ways when they are experiencing challenging emotions. I'll also explain why we actually make parenting much harder than it needs to be by trying to control our child's emotions.

If we help children to express themselves fully through crying (and laughter too), behaviour challenges then melt away, and your child can grow into a happy, well-adjusted adult who isn't weighed down with emotional baggage.

My Story

I always wanted to be a parent, but in my mid-twenties I wasn't in a happy place. My parents split up after 30 years of marriage and I was surprised that it affected me so strongly. I fell into a depression and began to reflect on my childhood. I always thought that I'd had a happy childhood, but now I wasn't so sure. I wondered if my parents had been unhappy for a long time and if their unhappiness had affected me. I had spent a large amount of my childhood being 'friends' with a group of girls who were actually more like bullies. I grew up lacking confidence. Now I started to feel a lot of anger. Why hadn't my parents separated sooner?

Since my teenage years, I had written journals, and always wrote when I felt upset, which helped me to feel better. This time, no matter how much I tried to express my feelings on the page, it didn't seem to help. I just felt stuck with my angry thoughts.

It was only when I got in touch with my body through meditation and yoga that I started to move beyond anger and find my real feelings of sadness. I cried a lot, a grief I'd never realised I'd carried before. That's when my real healing began. I was finally able to release my feelings instead of getting stuck with them.

At the time, I picked up a book by the spiritual teacher Osho, who said that our emotions are literally meant to be 'in motion'. When we fully feel our emotions, they can flow through us without becoming stagnant.[2]

Finally my emotions were starting to move, and I could let go of my anger and frustration, through finding the deeper sadness beneath. Afterwards, I discovered a more profound happiness, which comes from moving through sadness to the other side. I began to leave my childhood story behind and to live more in the present.

I started to live the kind of life I had always wanted, full of happiness, confidence and rewarding friendships. At the time, I had no idea that it was the tears that enabled me to transform my life. I would learn all about that later.

As I became happier, I began to think about becoming a parent. I'd always wanted to have children, but I had met so many people like me who spent their adult life trying to get over their childhood. Was there another way? I didn't realise at the time that I had already found it.

A few years earlier, my t'ai chi teacher, Michael, told me a story that sent me on a path towards a different way of parenting. He had been adopted and was quite a wild child. At one point he was sent to a remand centre, where somehow a Tibetan monk began taking care of him. Michael was engaging in his usual unruly behaviour, being disruptive and tearing the place apart. The monk reacted differently to Michael from most of the other adults. He didn't get angry or tell him to stop, he simply remained calm. Michael soon stopped behaving badly, and the monk even helped him to learn to read.

I have carried this story with me ever since. If we can regulate our own emotions, our children's natural goodness will shine through. Meditation, t'ai chi and yoga did help me to process my emotions in a healthy way, although by the time I was 30 I certainly hadn't found a state of perfect calm. Nevertheless, I did decide to have a child.

Just before becoming pregnant with my daughter, I was working as a babysitter for a five-year-old boy. The first few times I looked after him he had tantrums if we didn't have the kind of snack he wanted or when we had to leave the house quickly to go somewhere.

I didn't know what to do. I found myself thinking, *He's not a toddler; he shouldn't be having tantrums*. I assumed that there must be something wrong with him because he cried occasionally – it was the kind of judgement that only a non-parent can make.

I went home and googled 'what to do about tantrums'. I felt like I needed some kind of method to get them to stop. I read suggestions about using time out or ignoring the behaviour, but neither of these felt right to me. How could I ignore or punish a child who was clearly upset?

I googled a bit more and came across the idea of simply staying close, offering empathy and warmth, not using distraction to try to stop the child from crying but simply being there, until the tantrum was over.

It seemed so obvious, but I hadn't thought of it until I read those words. I actually didn't need to *do* anything. I just needed to be there, staying close until the storm had passed. There's something so unruly, so wild about tantrums that I felt that I needed some expert advice on how to handle them. But in actual fact, all I needed to do was follow my natural instinct to be a warm, loving caregiver.

A few months later I became pregnant and bought a book, called *The Aware Baby*, by Aletha Solter, which I'd seen recommended on the website about tantrums. I was simply intrigued by the title. The book explained how babies have a natural inborn mechanism for recovering from stress and upsets: crying. Solter explains that there are two reasons babies cry and how distinguishing between the two makes all the difference. The first reason, the most well-known one, is that babies cry simply to get their needs met. They can't use words, and so crying signals their need for food, warmth, closeness, and so on. The second reason is that babies also cry to heal from stressful experiences such as a difficult birth, medical intervention or just the everyday stress of being in a new, stimulating world.[3]

Reading about the healing power of tears was a revelation to me. I thought about all the things that had helped me heal and how they had all involved tears. I remembered how in creative-writing classes I'd taught, participants often wrote personal stories about their life and then started crying when they read their work aloud.

I remember how I often cried after having deep-tissue massages, which always left me feeling emotional as well as physically relaxed. They helped me get deep into the emotions stored in my body.

One of my friends trained in a type of energy healing called theta healing, and she practised with me as part of her training. Afterwards, I would often spend a few days at home writing, and crying. It was powerful and exhausting, but I always emerged feeling happier after moving through all my feelings.

I also tried a transformational breathing workshop – a deep-breathing practice that helps to release blockages in the body.

The workshop evoked powerful emotions in all the participants. At the end of the day everyone was holding hands and was moved to tears as we talked about our experiences in the workshop. Instinctively and intuitively I had found my own path to healing without even realising I was seeking my own tears.

This was the antidote to all my fears about parenting. It seemed amazing that there was a way we can bring up children so that they don't have to carry emotional baggage. We can help them to heal while they are still young so that they won't need to do so much soul-searching as adults.

When I next went to babysit for the boy I talked about earlier, he was recovering from flu. He had a Technical Lego set for age 7 and above and had started building a helicopter. He could actually follow most of the instructions to make it, but from time to time he would get stuck and need my help. Then we arrived at a step that neither of us could work out. Perhaps it was my 'pregnancy brain', but no matter how hard I stared at the instructions I couldn't understand what to do. He kept asking me over and over to help him, but I gently explained that I couldn't. He started to cry and tantrum, stamping his feet. I stayed with him for a few minutes. Then, as suddenly as he started, he stopped crying. He sat down again, and constructed the Lego himself.

This was such a wonderful example of how crying clears difficult feelings out of the mind so that we can think clearly again. When the boy had finished crying, his frustration was gone, so he could think clearly – and even better than he had done before the upset began.

If I had listened to my urge to persuade him to stop and do something else to distract him, I would never have witnessed what happens when we simply connect and listen, without trying to resolve the situation. What a wonderful lesson in confidence and independence that even without an adult to help he could still work things out for himself.

Becoming a parent – my first steps in listening

When my daughter was born, I discovered that listening to a baby's feelings was not always so straightforward. Like most new parents, I sometimes struggled to work out what she needed. There were times in the evening when I would be feeding her and she would keep coming off the breast. I would bounce her, pace the room with her, or try the wind-releasing pose from yoga on her, to try to get her to stop crying.

At other times there would be moments when I would remember what I'd learnt, that crying was healing, that perhaps she just needed to cry. I would sit down on the bed and just be with her, holding her and looking into her eyes.

Her birth had been difficult, a long induction where her heart rate had dropped low. Eventually, she had been born by vacuum extraction. I could think of no other reason why she would need to cry so much.

I found myself telling her that she was safe now, and that I was sorry it was hard coming into the world. It was heartbreaking to watch her cry so much, but I also felt a deep sense of connection with her in these moments. She was showing me her deepest pain, and I was there to help her let it go.

It really helped my confidence as a new mum to know that crying was OK, that sometimes my daughter would cry for what seemed like no apparent reason and that sometimes all she needed was for me to hold her in my arms and listen.

Yet I became confused about how I could work out if my daughter needed something or if she was crying to heal. I remember bouncing her around on the train and wondering if I was doing it because that's what she needed or if I felt some unspoken cultural pressure to keep her quiet. How would I know if she was hungry or physically uncomfortable, or if she was crying to heal? It seemed like quite a risk to get it wrong. If crying was healing, how come it only seemed to be this one book by Aletha Solter that said so? Why did no one else even mention the healing power of tears?

By the time my daughter was seven months old, she was hardly crying at all. She was a happy, relaxed baby, so on the surface everything was fine; however, she did still wake every two hours at night, which can be a sign of emotional tension. She co-slept in bed with me so I would fall straight back to sleep after feeding her, so I didn't think of it as a problem. But I couldn't simply forget what I'd learnt about the healing power of tears. If crying was a good thing, then shouldn't she at least be crying a bit? Was I somehow stopping her from crying without even consciously realising it?

I began to notice that when I fed her to sleep at night, she wriggled her body and seemed tense. I sensed I wasn't helping her relax. She always asked for milk before bed, although she was never really hungry. She was never really that hungry when she woke in the night either.

I began to realise that feeding to sleep and feeding her in the night had become a 'control pattern' – a habit to stop her from releasing her feelings by crying. One of the common reasons children wake in the night is because of emotional stress, just like adults do. She did need to cry.[4]

I started searching on the Internet for information about crying. I remembered an article my baby-massage teacher had given me by someone named Patty Wipfler – the one other person I'd heard was writing about crying to heal. I googled her and discovered her parenting website, Hand in Hand.[5] On the website I found an article all about breastfeeding. I was relieved to hear Patty's compassionate advice: it's natural that in the close breastfeeding relationship children often come to depend on the breast for comfort. She explains how we can begin to work out the times when what our babies actually need is to cry.

I decided to take what felt like a leap. Before naps and at bedtime I stopped breastfeeding my daughter or bouncing her, or putting her to sleep in a sling or a buggy. I didn't leave her alone to self-soothe by using a dummy or sucking her thumb. I just held her and stayed with her. She had some big cries – more powerful now that I wasn't doing something to distract her from her feelings.

At first I constantly questioned whether it was really OK just to let her cry. It felt isolating that I had no one to talk to about the process, but it no longer seemed right to continue to stop her from crying when I had experienced the benefits of healing tears first hand.

Then I saw the way she looked after she cried. She was so peaceful, as if she had been doing some baby yoga or meditation. After a big cry, she always fell asleep easily. It was no longer a battle with me doing something to make her fall asleep. I was simply being there with her, allowing her to tell me how she was feeling. When she fell asleep, she would often smile and even giggle sometimes as she fell into dreams. It was clear that once I let go of the pattern of stopping her feelings she was free to cry away her upset, and find real contentment.

Developing listening as children grow

I began listening to my daughter in the night, slowly dropping the feeds one by one. I would hold her and listen to her feelings instead. She began sleeping better, waking less, and her sleep was much deeper. She would no longer wake at the slightest noise or movement. It was as if she had internalised a sense of safety so she didn't need to sleep lightly and restlessly, always checking that I was there. Now she actually felt safe. The fearful times were over; she had let out her feelings, so now she could relax, trusting that I was there for her.

When I first became a mother and spent my time reading baby books and searching the Internet, knowing that I wanted to parent peacefully, I had one unanswered question in my mind: how could I control behaviour? What if I needed my daughter to do something, or if I needed to stop her from doing something?

If I was nice and gentle to her all the time, how could I set limits with her?

I read a story on the Hand in Hand Parenting blog, about a toddler who had developed a fear of the bath. The mother didn't know what to do, apart from ignoring the feelings and forcing him into the bath or avoiding giving him a bath at all. Then one day she realised she could listen to his feelings. That evening she gently told him he needed to take a bath. He started to cry. She held him and listened to him for a while, gently reminding him, from time to time, that he did need to take a bath. Then he finished crying. She put his bath toys into the bath, and when he saw his crab swimming he decided he wanted to get in too.[6]

This is how parenting can work when we start listening. We don't need to parent by force. When our children are free of upset feelings, we can work things through together and find a way of cooperating together.

Listening to my daughter's feelings helped her to be a happy, calm baby who grew into a happy, relaxed toddler. As she grew older, there would be times when she'd get grumpy, or refuse to do things like have her nappy changed or get dressed. I'd find myself thinking: *Oh, the terrible twos are coming.* Then I'd realise that my daughter was feeling stressed due to travelling or other changes and upheaval. I'd connect with her. We'd spend time laughing and being close to each other. Then she'd release feelings with a big cry and the challenging behaviour would disappear. The 'terrible twos' never came. There are periods when life is harder than others, but we always get back on track when I connect with her and listen to her feelings.

I remember once, at a family party, my daughter had been relaxed and happy for the whole afternoon. My mother-in-law's friend (a mother of four grown-up children) said to me, 'I have no idea what you're doing, but just keep doing it.' It was the best validation I could have asked for that listening to our children's tears allows them to be their natural, good and cooperative selves.

My healing journey continues

When I saw an advert that Hand in Hand were looking for instructor trainees, I felt a strong urge to sign up, not really knowing why, but just that I thought their ideas were amazing and I wanted to share them with others. This is why I decided to write this book. Friends or relatives would sometimes assume that my daughter never cried, because she was often so relaxed and happy. I wanted to share with others that it wasn't that she didn't cry but that when she did I had learnt a simple way of listening. I wasn't stopping or fixing her feelings; instead, she could fully release her upset every time and return to her natural, joyful self.

As part of my Hand in Hand Parenting training I started something called a listening partnership: a way that parents themselves can share and release feelings about how parenting is going, through talking, laughing and crying, in person or via phone or Skype.

At the time, I thought I had already done all my healing before becoming a mother. I loved being a mum and I was really happy. But when I started my first listening partnership, with a listening partner that I found through Hand in Hand, I realised that a lot of the emotions I thought were an inevitable part of parenting – the stress and the exhaustion, the desperately wanting time to myself – were all emotions I could release simply by talking about them. I would start a listening time feeling like I needed a break from parenting for hours or even days. Then, ten minutes after my listening session on Skype, I'd bounce back into the room where my daughter was, completely re-energised, feeling the joy of being in her presence again.

At first I didn't cry. I didn't think it would be possible to cry in front of anyone except my husband or when I was alone. But nine months into my listening partnership, I began to open up with my listening partner and cry about things long buried in the past. That's when I realised that it is actually possible to catch up on the crying we didn't do as children, so that the memories no longer affect our present. Our healing process is ongoing; there are always stories to tell and tears to shed. We can always improve our sense of well-being.

When I was listened to, it became a lot easier for me to listen to my daughter. My mind was a lot clearer when it wasn't full of the clutter of unheard feelings from my own childhood. I now have the patience and clarity of mind to listen to her cry, always accepting that even if she is crying about something petty, like being given a cup in the wrong colour or having a broken biscuit, there is probably a deeper reason for the upset.

Healing our children; healing ourselves

Listening to tears is not easy. This is an approach that starts with putting on our own oxygen mask first: in aeroplane safety instructions parents are always recommended to put on their own oxygen mask before helping a child with theirs. This is a metaphor that applies to parenting too. We need to get emotional support before we support our children with their strong emotions, to catch up on the listening we didn't get as children. When we were young, few of us experienced what it was like to have our feelings really listened to. When we were babies, we were rocked or shushed, or left alone to cry, and as we grew older, we may have been gently redirected from crying, distracted, ignored, reprimanded, told that 'big boys don't cry', or even 'Don't cry or I'll give you something to cry about.'

We can feel at a loss as to what to do when our children cry. It triggers our own unconscious memories of how people responded to us when we cried. We may never have experienced being listened to until the end of a big cry. Although people may have treated us with kindness or compassion, they probably actively tried to stop us from crying before we'd fully released our upset, even if it was done gently.

When it comes to our own children, we often feel compelled to do the same, sometimes without being aware of it. This is what I did when my daughter was young, even though I knew tears were healing.

It's our own history and cultural attitudes to crying that have kept this information hidden and unknown to the majority of parents. These attitudes are often so strong that even reading about the healing power of tears isn't always enough to actually learn what it means to fully listen.

This is why the purpose of this book is not only to share important information about crying; it also has a strong practical component with exercises and techniques to try so that we can bring our own reaction to tears into our conscious awareness. Then we can finally undo our own unconscious patterns to stop our children from expressing their feelings, and allow them instead to heal in the way that nature intended.

Walking along life's road with your child

This is a healing path that you and your child can walk together – one that involves not just listening to upsets but also to laughter, joy and a deep sense of connection. It is possible to stay close to your children into the teen years, and beyond.

This book is like a roadmap for you to begin to listen to your child, and recover your own lost tears. In each chapter there are exercises to help you reflect on your childhood and your current parenting challenges. There are tips and techniques to build emotional closeness so that your child can release the old hurts that cause challenging behaviour. I'll also show you how to set limits and create boundaries in a way that actually builds more closeness between you and your child.

Because life is often full of challenges that are beyond our control, I'll show you how to repair broken connections from the times when it was hard to be fully present with your child, such as when a new sibling arrives, or when we experience illness, divorce or bereavement. Because we have this recovery process that rebuilds closeness, it's never too late to start listening to tears.

Recovering your lost tears as an adult is immensely beneficial and can transform your life. To allow your child to heal while they're still young is the greatest gift you can give them. I hope you and your family enjoy walking this healing path together.

A big part of this process is getting support for yourself as a parent. At the end of each chapter of this book there are exercises that ask you to reflect on your own parenting and childhood. Ideally, it's great if you can find a friend or listening partner to talk through your answers. As you create safety and trust with your partner, you can release some of your own backlog of feelings and recover your energy and enthusiasm for parenting. If you want to start straight away, writing in a notebook can also help. Here is the first exercise, which asks you to think about what makes you, and other people, cry.

EXERCISE: **Reflection – thinking about what makes you cry**

1   Do you find it easy to cry? Under what circumstances or with whom do you cry the most easily?

2   What about the people around you? Have you noticed if they cry easily, or is crying more difficult for them? Why do you think that might be?

3   What songs and films make you cry? Rent a few tearjerkers, and put on some sad music. Let the tears flow without holding back.

CHAPTER 1

The Stories That Lead Us to Tears

•

'Tears are words waiting to be written.'

Paulo Coelho

When the founder of Hand in Hand Parenting, Patty Wipfler, was a young mother, she met a younger acquaintance who asked her what being a parent was like. Patty burst into tears. She explained that although she had always loved children, parenting was so much more exhausting and stressful than she thought it would be. She confessed that she was starting to lose her temper, being aggressive towards her children in a similar way to how she had been treated as a child. As Patty talked, and cried, the woman just listened.

Afterwards, Patty went home and found that she felt completely different. She had much more energy and renewed patience to be with her children again. When Patty next met the young woman, Patty asked her what she had done. The woman explained to Patty about the simple method of listening she had used and how it can help us to release our feelings.

Patty began taking classes in listening and exchanging listening time with another parent. She explored how simply talking about her feelings, laughing, crying and reflecting on her own childhood helped her to remove the emotional obstacles that were standing in the way of her being the parent she wanted to be.

Storytelling: the key to successful parenting

Telling your own life story is a fundamental element of bringing up happy, emotionally resilient children. What Patty discovered intuitively is now supported by the latest research: a study conducted by the University of Berkeley showed that the more coherent a story of our own childhood we can tell, the better attached our children will be to us. The researchers found that it's not what happens in our childhood that determines how we parent but how we make sense of our own life story.

The researchers defined a coherent story as one that went beyond simple labels like 'happy' or 'terrible' but which went into more detail. Coherent stories combined events and emotions in a way that made sense, rather than describing events without the person's emotional reactions, or giving emotional responses without clearly explaining the events that caused them. The study found that telling a coherent story is the single most important factor that determines how well our children are attached to us. The research also found that the parts of our stories that we struggle to talk about coherently relate to the parts of our adult life where we have difficulties.[1]

When it comes to parenting, history often repeats itself, even when we don't intend it to. We can have the best of intentions to be 'perfect' parents, but we can find ourselves losing control and reacting in ways that we are not proud of, particularly when our children do things that push our buttons. This almost always happens when we are feeling stressed and exhausted.

In *Parenting from the Inside Out*, professor of psychiatry Daniel J. Siegel explains what happens in the brain when we become stressed. The limbic system (the emotion centre of the brain) becomes flooded with emotion, while the pre-frontal cortex (the rational, thinking part of the brain that governs impulse control) becomes deactivated.

When our child does something that pushes our buttons,

such as dropping food on the floor on purpose or hitting a sibling, it can trigger unconscious memories of our own childhood and how we were treated in similar situations. These memories activate our own strong emotions, so it's hard to think clearly in the moment. We may respond in an automatic way, rather than thinking through our response. We may simply repeat what our parents did to us when we were children. '

Telling our stories helps us to diffuse some of the potency of the past. We can fully process and release our emotions about our own experiences, so that we are no longer reliving them in the present. Then, when we find ourselves in a stressful situation with our children, we can bring ourselves back to emotional equilibrium and think clearly about how to respond.

The key ingredient in storytelling

Crying is an essential part of this process of storytelling. A research study showed that people in therapy were found to recover better and make more positive changes in their lives when they cried during their sessions.[2] Through crying we can release the emotional charge from our experiences so that we can make sense of what happened and tell our stories more coherently.

When we have a supportive listener, and the safety and space to tell our stories, we will be led to our tears. It might not happen instantly, as we have all to some extent developed patterns of trying to hold in our feelings. But, over time, we can recover our natural healing ability. We might cry about memories long buried in the past, events we didn't even know we were upset about. Our true feelings emerge about things we might have borne with a brave face, or felt numb about. Writer and creative writing teacher Louise DeSalvo describes the recovery of feelings like these as 'the things we would have felt at the time if we weren't so afraid'.[3]

Unshed tears: the story we all need to tell

I grew up thinking that I didn't have much of a life story to tell. I had thought of myself as having a happy, normal childhood, although I was often drawn to people who had 'suffered'. I had friends whose parents had been violent or had addictions. If I compared my past to theirs, it felt like I had nothing to complain about.

I remember being at a party of writers and we were talking about whether it was necessary to suffer to be a writer. I remember saying, 'Oh, I had a happy childhood – it's just that I'm sensitive.' I had heard one of my writer friends using the label 'sensitive' and it seemed a good choice to explain my writer's sensibility. But it didn't actually explain anything about my childhood and why certain aspects of my adult life were hard.

When my parents separated, it was the trigger for me to begin to look closely at my childhood story. I gained a deeper understanding of my upbringing that went beyond those simple labels of 'normal' and 'happy'.

We are taught to minimise our feelings, to say everything's fine and to put on a brave face. Our childhood had a sense of normalcy because we didn't know any different at the time. As adults, we can reflect more consciously on our past.

When I learnt about the healing power of tears, I realised that none of us were able to cry freely as children. We all have crying to catch up on. It's not as simple as dividing up humanity into those who had traumatic childhoods and those who had happy ones. We can all benefit from reflecting on our own life histories and releasing some of the feelings we've been carrying. Each time we do so we strengthen and deepen the attachment with our children because our past hurts are no longer standing in the way of us being the parents we want to be.

How's parenting going?

To begin to discover the benefits of telling your story, find a friend or begin a listening partnership through the Hand in Hand Parenting community, either online or in your local area (see the Appendix on page 253).

For a quick experiment to try out the power of listening, you and your friend, or listening partner, can spend five minutes talking and then five minutes listening each. This is a sample taster to try out the skills with a friend and to demonstrate the power that just a short amount of listening time can bring, as we saw in the experiences of Patty Wipfler I described earlier.

You ask each other this simple question, 'How is parenting going?'

When listening, try not to interrupt, give advice or tell your own stories while the other person is talking. Remember not to judge the other person on their difficulties but focus instead on listening as they tell their story. Make an agreement to keep everything you say confidential and do not refer to it outside the session. I discuss these basic guidelines in more detail in Chapter 4.

You might not burst into tears like Patty did, but you will start to create the space and safety to listen to your own feelings. You can also discover how your present actions relate to the past.

When parents begin a listening partnership, they often start by telling their life story. Exchanging time talking and listening is a wonderful way to get to know someone or to deepen an existing relationship. It's advisable not to do this with your spouse, at least while you're beginning to learn the listening process, as things can get heated when you are both so emotionally involved with your children.

Beginning your story

To start a listening partnership, set aside 30–45 minutes each and begin to tell your story in a stream-of-consciousness style: you can jump from memory to memory like stepping stones, simply following wherever your mind takes you.

Writing your life story down can also be an effective way to process your thoughts and create a coherent chain of events. You might want to try that as you work through this book, if you are finding it takes some time to discover a listening partnership that works for you. Ideally, however, it's best to have a listening partner. That way when you feel emotional you have someone right there to laugh and cry with. Because we have a history of hiding away our emotions, of being sent to our rooms or being told not to cry, it is a powerful antidote to have someone there who really accepts us unconditionally, whatever we're going through.

Another way of using a listening partnership is to think of the areas of your life that you're struggling with right now. It could be to do with parenting or other aspects of your life that you'd like to change. Or it could be the things that trigger you about your child, that make you lose patience or feel stressed and over-whelmed. Anything that triggers strong feelings in you is likely to relate to a hurt from the past. Make a note of them as potential topics to talk about. You can ask yourself (or a listening partner can ask you) if this situation reminds you of anything in the past and how you were treated as a child. If we trace our present issues back to the past and release the emotion we've been carrying, we can think more clearly about how to deal with the present.

The pain of the past

When my daughter turned two I began noticing that she was sometimes shy around people she didn't know. This is a common response for a toddler, but it made me worried that she'd end up like I was as a child, being bullied and struggling to make good friends. I would talk about it in my listening time, simply describing whatever memories came into my mind. When I was aged seven or eight years old I tried to block out my emotions about what was happening and just not think about it. I remember thinking I had invented a trick in my mind that if something wasn't nice, I could just choose not to think about it.

As an adult, in my listening partnership, I began to recall all the things that had happened. The girls would always pull my hairband out and hide it. They'd make me do 'chores' for them, like putting their lunch boxes away. We'd play leapfrog and they'd always push me over instead of leaping over me, even though they promised not to. They'd spend time styling my hair, brushing and yanking it until it hurt. One of the bullies broke a pen that I'd saved up to buy with my pocket money.

As I talked to my listening partner, the emotion of what happened welled up in me, and I started crying. My listening partner provided the safety for me to release feelings I'd been carrying around with me ever since the bullying.

Every time I talked about it I shed a few more of those old feelings. I noticed that after a listening partnership little pieces of my confidence came back. I became less and less shy, and more comfortable with myself. I also worried less about my daughter becoming shy. Without my own upset feelings in the way, I could think more clearly about how to help her.

Introducing playlistening

Shortly after I'd talked a lot about my experience of being bullied, we were at the house of a new friend I'd recently made. Her two-year-old son was running in and out of the room. My daughter sat on my lap sucking her fingers, a sure sign that she was feeling nervous. I played a game where I pretended to be scared of the boy too. Every time he ran past, I'd jump back with my daughter, saying 'Oooo!' Soon she was laughing. This is one of the listening tools I had learnt in my Hand in Hand Parenting training: playlistening.

Playlistening means finding something that will make our child laugh while we, the parent, adopt a less powerful role, as above when I pretended to be scared. We repeat the action over and over to get the giggles going. When I pretended to be scared, my daughter began to feel powerful, and the laughter helped her to release some of her nervous tension. After a few more minutes playing this game, my daughter was happy to go and play trains with her new friend, and they got on really well for the rest of the afternoon.

That day I was feeling relaxed and confident myself. I was able to leave my own past behind, and focus on what my daughter needed in the present. If I hadn't reflected on my own childhood, I'd have just been sitting there feeling as nervous as she was, and wouldn't have been able to help her. My daughter would have probably picked up on my feelings and felt even more uncomfortable. Having been able to release my own feelings about shyness I was able to help her grow in confidence too.

Our children are our greatest teachers. They will find the places where we need to work out more about ourselves and our past. Parenting is a chance to grow and sparkle, to be our best selves. Having a rich understanding of our own emotional lives lays the foundation for having the empathy and patience to cope with our children's strong emotions. Through the challenges we deal with, the laughter and tears along the way, we become the parents our children need us to be.

Our children's stories

Our children want to be close to us and tell us their stories. They want us to know what's going on in their lives. They want to have a good cry with us – from infancy through to their teenage years. It's a common misconception that as our children grow older they will inevitably turn more towards their peer groups for emotional support. If we can keep listening, keep accepting their feelings and dealing with our own, we can keep the emotional connection with them, even as they grow in independence, build friendships and set off into the world. Many parents who have used the Hand in Hand approach have experienced close relationships with their children into the teenage years and beyond.

An infant's first language is crying. They cry to express needs and also to heal from upsets. Babies have lots to tell us. They cry to process many big and small experiences, as they get used to being in this new, stimulating world. It's natural for a baby to have big cries every day in their first year of life.

As new parents, we can feel nervous and anxious, trying to work out what our baby needs. It can feel like life and death, being responsible for this brand-new little person. We want to be absolutely sure that they have all their needs met.

Healing stories

It's also important to bear in mind that our baby's crying is not always a demand to put something right in the present. Sometimes it's a way to tell a story about the past – and recover from it.

One day when my daughter was a young baby, we were out walking and my neighbour appeared from around the corner. My daughter was startled and suddenly started crying. She continued to cry even after the neighbour had disappeared into her house. Everything was fine in the present: she was safe with me. I was calm and reassured her, but that sudden moment had given her a fright, and her body had gone into fight-or-flight mode – the body's natural way of getting ready to respond to danger, which involves releasing stress hormones. When she knew it was safe again, she could recover through crying.

In this example, the scary, upsetting moment was only a few seconds before my daughter cried. Babies might also have a big cry at the end of the day to release any stress or overstimulation from that day. Stress in pregnancy, a traumatic birth, or medical interventions can also cause babies to cry a lot. In one study Dr Päivi Tuire Rautava, a Finnish paediatrician, found that women who had problems or stress during pregnancy, or who had difficult birth experiences, were more likely to have babies who cried a lot.[4]

Babies don't always get a chance to cry freely, so they gather an emotional backpack of experiences that they can carry throughout childhood and into adulthood. We can help make this backpack as light as possible by learning how to listen to their tears.

Our children might cry about things weeks, months or even years after they have happened. As my adult examples show, we can still heal from our childhood when we are much older.

One morning, when my daughter was two, she woke up crying powerfully. I wondered what had happened. Did she have a bad dream? I went into our bedroom and sat holding her, rather than rushing out with her and trying to distract her with something. I'd been listening to her upsets since she was a newborn, simply accepting that there was a reason behind them, even though she couldn't verbalise it yet.

That morning, halfway through her crying she exclaimed, 'Mummy dropped me!' I knew she was referring to an incident at the swimming pool a few days before. She had jumped into the water, and I had been there to catch her, but, for a split second, she slipped through my fingers. Her head had gone under water, and then I caught her.

I gently reassured her that she was safe now, that I had caught her after that. I was careful not to interfere with her telling of the story. I let her cry to release all the fear that she must have been carrying around with her since the incident. When she stopped crying, I explained that she had gone underwater for a split second, but I had caught her straight away. I told her she had always been safe. Together, we rebuilt a story of the incident so that she could understand that although it had felt scary at the time, I had kept her safe.

At that time my daughter had been going through a phase of being afraid of slides. Later that day, she went down a slide in the park. I'm sure the big cry helped her to release some fear, so she could feel confident to try something new.

This was the first time in her life that she'd told me what had happened. All those other times she had cried she was processing upsetting experiences, even if she couldn't tell me about them.

How we express emotion

The language of emotion is a non-verbal one. The limbic system – the home of emotion in the brain – is fully formed before birth, whereas the pre frontal cortex – the home of language – is not fully developed until adulthood.[5] Even our adult pre-frontal cortex doesn't function well when we are overwhelmed by emotion. As adults we often find it hard to put our feelings into words. As our children get older and can express their needs with words, they still need to cry.

Releasing the raw emotions is part of the process of making sense of things. When a child cries, they are expressing a word-less story of why they feel so bad. They might include some words or they might say nothing at all. When the limbic system resets itself, and calm has been re-established, our child can access their pre-frontal cortex more easily. They can then talk about what happened, and we can help them piece together a story.

When we pick up our toddler from nursery and ask them how their day was, they may not say anything at all, but they do tell us how they are feeling through their behaviour. If they had a hard day, they'll start moaning and whining, tantrumming or hitting a sibling.

Common parenting wisdom suggests we give our child a punishment or consequence of some sort for this kind of 'misbehaviour'; however, when a child is upset, their pre-frontal cortex isn't working well and they find it hard to control their impulses. Punishments and consequences disconnect the child further and send a clear message that we don't want to know what they are going through. Further disconnection will result in more off-track behaviour (see box), or the child will learn that their parent isn't there to listen to their emotions.

Instead of interpreting your child's behaviour as 'bad', you can see it as a message. He or she is waving a red flag to you saying, 'I need to tell you something!' They may be behaving in challenging ways because they can't think how to tell you clearly.

We need to connect with them, and give them the opportunity to tell their story, while setting limits on their behaviour in a gentle, loving way. It would be very off-putting if we sat down in front of them and said, 'Right then, I'm here to listen. Let's talk!' This puts pressure on them to give us information that they can't verbalise when they are in the feeling mode.

Emotions tend to come out in their own time and space. Our job is to provide a safe arena for them and give our child a clear non-verbal message that we are listening and that we want to know what's going on in their lives.

I discuss playlistening in more detail in Chapter 11.

Off-track behaviour

Throughout this book I won't use the terms 'bad behaviour' or 'misbehaviour' to describe when our child is acting in ways that aren't acceptable. These descriptions often imply that the responsibility is on the child to fix their own behaviour. Science now shows that children lack impulse control when they are

▶

upset because the pre-frontal cortex of their brain can't function as well. I will therefore use the term 'off-track' to describe when our child is acting in ways that indicate they have some upset feelings that they need our help to listen to.

Introducing special time

The Hand in Hand Parenting tool of special time gives children the message that we are listening. To do special time, set a timer for a short period of time, say 10 or 15 minutes, and tell your child that they can do whatever they like. If you have more than one child, find a time when someone else can take care of your other children.

Special time is a little bit different from the regular quality time we spend with our children, because for this period we try not to put any limits on our child, apart from ensuring their safety.

Special time gives your child a space to lap up your warm attention. When they have it, they might give you a hint of what they are going through. When my daughter was two, she always chose to go outside and play with her dolls. She would carry them along the path and then suddenly drop them and run off. I would act in the voice of her babies, saying 'Mummy, mummy, mummy!' then pick up the babies and run after her. She would run away laughing, and I would always let her get away.

Special time often becomes an opportunity for playlistening. In the above situation, my daughter got to be the all-powerful mummy who was leaving, while I was cast in the role of the helpless baby. Telling this story of a mummy leaving helped her to make sense of the times when I needed to leave, and it also helped her deal with separation anxiety.

Through laughter and play, children can tell us their stories.

When we listen, join in and stay close, we build safety so that they can cry with us when they need to.

Just like adults, children may find tears as they tell their stories. It might be during the play; for example, when my daughter was running away from her babies, she might fall over and bump her knee, crying hard (even though the physical hurt was small). Or after an evening full of giggles she might wake up crying. Or later, when I needed to go out and leave her with her dad, she might have a big cry about separation.

When tears come, it can seem like the fun games have turned sour. But if we look below the surface, these kinds of tears aren't negative. There's nothing really wrong in the present moment. Our child has had our warmth and attention, and feels full up with love.

If everything's well in the present, it's likely that our child is releasing an upset from the past. When this happens, all we need to do is listen. The more we listen and connect with our children, the more they will tell us, and this investment in time pays off. Our children will need to tell us less, and less through off-track behaviour. The whining, hitting and behaviour that can drive us crazy will disappear, replaced with play, laughter and, sometimes, tears.

Case Study: Claire

'I was in the supermarket with my four-year-old when she asked me to buy her some chocolate. She had been quite grumpy and whiny before that, so I sensed that something was bothering her. I said no, and she started crying. After about ten minutes, she started saying, "Don't put that girl in the corner." I listened to her for a while, and then later, when she'd finished crying, I asked her what she meant. It turned out that they'd been using time out in the Kindergarten, and that it had upset her.

'Although I wasn't happy that the Kindergarten were using time out, I was glad that I'd said no to the chocolate, as it gave me the opportunity to listen to my daughter in a deeper way and work out what was bothering her. She was in a much better mood after that, so I think to some extent she healed some of the hurt and upset from seeing another child being punished.'

In this case study you'll see that when a parent has a difficulty with their child it's not the parent's fault but a reflection of how they've been hurt. Telling their story can help them make changes to their parenting.

Case Study: David

'When my son John was three, I started really struggling to be the kind of parent I wanted to be. John was hitting me a lot and I was struggling to connect with him. During a listening time my partner asked me, "Who does John remind you of?" I realised that he reminded me of my dad, who had hit me when I was young. In the listening time I went back to my childhood and recalled the times my father had hit me. It was like reliving the situation, except now I had a listening partner to support me, as I cried and raged. I was able to get angry at my father, which I never could have done at the time. Fighting back gave me new strength. When my son lashed out aggressively, I could handle it in a more playful way. We had a lot of fun playing rough-and-tumble. The old feelings weren't standing in the way of connecting any more. My relationship with my son got better and better.'

EXERCISE: Reflection – tell your life story

The best way to do this is with a listener.

1   Divide the time and take turns to talk and listen.

2   Jump from memory to memory, following your stream of consciousness.

EXERCISE: Focus on parenting

1   Write down three things you liked about the way you were parented.

2   Write down three things that you would do differently.

3   Talk about these with a listening partner.

4   What behaviour in your children evokes a strong reaction in you? Vent about these feelings with a listening partner.

EXERCISE: Try this – special time and playlistening

1   Set a timer and let your child choose what to do for 10–15 minutes – this is special time, which I explain in more detail in Chapter 10.

2   Playlistening: have a giggle-fest with your child or children, and pick up on what makes them laugh while they take on the more powerful role. (Don't tickle though, as this can make children feel powerless and overwhelmed.) I explain playlistening in more detail in Chapter 11.

CHAPTER 2

The Presence of a Listener – the Lighthouse in the Storm

•

'I want to write about the great and powerful
thing that listening is. And how we forget it.
And how we don't listen to our children, or those
we love. And least of all – which is so important,
too – to those we do not love. But we should.
Because listening is a magnetic and strange thing,
a creative force ... When we are listened to,
it creates us, makes us unfold and expand.
Ideas actually begin to grow within us
and come to life.'

Brenda Ueland, *The Art of Listening*

Listening to tears is about being a calm presence for our children. We can be like a lighthouse that can help to guide them through their stormy emotions. A lighthouse doesn't have the power to change the weather, but it does offer a point our children can use to locate themselves so that they feel safe and connected, even while they are overwhelmed with emotion. Guided by the lighthouse they can find their way out of the storm.

Listening to our children – introducing staylistening

When our children are upset, they always need a listener. There are mirror neurons in the brain that actually recreate and mirror the moods of those around us. When we are relaxed and loving, our child can release all his bad feelings and then attune to our brain, soak up our calm state and restore his own emotional equilibrium.[1]

Our children can't do it without us, and they can't do it while we're in emotional turmoil ourselves. To heal from the past, our child needs to know that all is well in the present. This is what Hand in Hand Parenting calls staylistening, which simply means staying close and listening to our child, until they are ready to stop crying.

This approach is very different from the 'cry it out' method where babies are left alone to cry. Crying it out results in an increase in stress hormones, probably because the baby or child feels abandoned and in immediate danger. Researcher Wendy Middlemiss at the University of Texas found that babies who were left alone to cry it out still had raised cortisol levels hours later.[2]

On the other hand, when we stay close to our children and listen to their emotional upsets, they can release stress hormones that have built up from upsetting experiences in the past.

Why just being present is so helpful

Scientific research has found that the brain is not really a solitary organ, but works in a system with the brains of other people around us, sending out and picking up subtle, non-verbal cues.[3] Because of the mirror neurons in the brain, just being there and thinking well of someone has a positive effect on how they feel.

Just being there, just holding the thought that crying and

tantrums are not bad behaviour but an expression of feelings is enough. It's a powerful boost to our child's self-esteem to sense that we still think they are a good person, even when they're having an emotional upset. Being a calm presence for our child lets them know that even if they've experienced something scary and upsetting they're safe now and can let all the feelings go.

When your child gets to the end of their emotions and emerges on the other side, they'll be brighter, stronger and more resilient, knowing that they possess everything they need to cope with their feelings. The gift of listening is actually the most powerful thing we can give to our children.

Crying is not a negative reflection on your parenting. It's actually a positive sign that your child feels safe enough to tell you about their big feelings. Once those feelings are gone, they won't need to tell you about them with off-track behaviour.

We can change our perception of crying, undo our cultural programming that it's something negative and recognise the times when it's a healthy, natural, healing process. Even amidst an emotional upset, things are getting better – your child is beginning to heal. That awareness can help you to stay calm in the moment.

When my daughter is crying, I always remind myself that when the emotional storm is over she'll be feeling much better. I've seen the results and know it's always worth investing the time to listen. I've seen how she grows in confidence in new and surprising ways, like hugging her best friend for the first time or exploring the park much further than before. I've seen how she whines and shouts less and is more affectionate with me.

One morning after a big cry, she gave me a big hug and said, 'I like mummy.' I knew she was grateful that I listened. She was very huggy that morning, but not in the clingy, 'I don't have the confidence to let you go' kind of way that toddlers have, which can really grate on our nerves. Her hugs were warm and relaxed.

After a big cry, it feels like the air has cleared for both of us, that any tension gathering in our relationship is gone and we feel really closely connected. Afterwards, her behaviour is less off-track, so I don't get so annoyed or stressed out, and parenting is much more fun.

How to staylisten

When your child becomes upset, you should first assess the situation. Does she need something? You need to check the obvious: is she hungry, thirsty or in danger? This is especially important with babies. As parents, we're always the best experts on our children and we should always trust our instincts.

There are many situations where we cannot fix what is wrong in our child's world; for example, she starts crying when mummy goes to work, or she is upset because a friend wouldn't play with her at pre-school, or because we need to set a limit about something unavoidable, such as when it's time to get out of the bath or to get ready to leave the house.

To staylisten you simply need to be there when your child cries, to offer closeness, connection, eye contact and kind, reassuring words. You shouldn't try to stop the crying, but just be there for as long as they need you to be. If your child is angry or tantrumming, and doesn't seem to want you, stay nearby nevertheless, letting them know that they can have a hug if they need one.

Staylistening involves a little talking, but not too much. You can gently reassure your child, saying things like, 'You're safe; I'm here for you', or if you are setting a limit, you can empathise with them saying, 'I'm sorry, we have to go now.'

This probably sounds quite obvious doesn't it? Listening to crying is a deep instinct we have. But for most of our lives it has become buried and tangled up with our own childhood history of not being listened to. Few of us were ever listened to until the end of a big cry, and so this instinct does not immediately come naturally to us.

We can fall into the assumption that it's our job to stop the crying as quickly as possible and that this equates with a happy child. If we can't fix the situation by mummy staying home that day, perhaps we can find some kind of substitute solution, such as a biscuit or a trip to the park to cheer her up.

These substitute solutions don't address the feelings underneath but merely mask them. The feelings are still there, and they might come out later in further upsets or off-track behaviour. Of course, we want to do nice things for our kids and create happy memories, but we need to allow them their sadness too.

Why using distractions doesn't work

In the long term, trying to actively make our children happy with substitute solutions trains them to run away from their feelings. They get into habits of seeking food, entertainment or other distractions, and become more and more out of touch with themselves. This creates the kind of habits that most of us adults have that we use to mask our feelings, using food, alcohol, keeping busy, and so on, in an attempt to replace the genuine sense of well-being we have lost. In Chapter 5 I'll cover more about how we can become aware of the ways we stop our children from crying and how we try to repress our own feelings with food or by other means. For now, we'll focus on what it really means to be a listener.

We want to let our children know that we are comfortable with their feelings, and that feelings are not something scary that they need to run away from. This allows them to fully heal and return to their natural, cooperative selves.

Sometimes, parents have a tendency to talk a lot when their children are upset, to ask them what's wrong or to ask them to explain verbally what the issue is: for example, if our child is upset about a friendship at pre-school, we might try to get to the root of this upset as quickly as possible. We'll try to work out who's in the right and who's in the wrong, if there's bullying going on, or if the teachers need to get involved, and so on.

When a child (or even an adult) is upset, it's actually quite hard to talk and work things out using words when they are caught up in their emotions. It can be hard for a child to explain what's wrong or to listen clearly to our reasoning when their pre-frontal cortex isn't working well.

Talking too much can pull a child away from their feelings, into the rational brain, before they've fully released the upset. It's hard for them to accept ways to resolve things or think about solutions when they still have a lot of feelings about the situation.

Your child might verbalise their upset while they're crying. We should try not to say much in response and not say more than a sentence or two, now and again. Our focus should be on listening and allowing them to talk or cry. They might say things that don't make much sense, or they might lash out with words, saying, 'I hate you mummy!' We should try to stay calm and not respond negatively to what they're saying, or try to reason them out of these thoughts. In many cases it might not really be them talking but the hurt feelings. Once the hurt feelings are gone, they won't think like this anymore.

The calm after the storm

When your child has fully released their upset, they can naturally restore their emotional equilibrium and start thinking clearly again. It will then be much easier to talk things through, and your child might even come up with their own solution to the situation. Even though our children are young, they are often the experts on their lives, and they might surprise you with a solution, just like the boy I babysat for who managed to build his Lego peacefully after he was upset.

Sometimes what appears to be a problem when the upset begins isn't really a problem at all, but is just a trigger to release some feelings. One evening, when my daughter was nine months old, my husband came home from work and went over to say hello to where she was happily playing on the floor. She burst into tears, and when my husband picked her up she reached out her arms for me.

I was surprised that she'd cried so suddenly. We had just spent a day full of lovely connection. She wasn't a newborn anymore. It seemed as if she'd been in the world long enough to understand that this was her dad, and she was in a completely safe situation. I was right next to her on her play-mat too.

I concluded that this tiny separation from me was triggering bigger fears. I decided not to pick her up. Instead I moved close to her and reassured her that she was safe with her dad and that I was there too. He held her as she cried, and we both gave her lots of warm loving attention. After a few minutes she stopped crying as suddenly as she'd started. She smiled, started babbling and pointing things out around the room. She was completely at ease being with her dad.

We had dinner and she tried two new foods that she had always refused before – potatoes and cheese. Releasing the separation fears helped her to be more adventurous.

If I had simply taken my daughter from my husband's arms, it would have been a kind of reflex action simply to stop her from crying. I would have fixed the situation, but I wouldn't have listened to what she really needed to say or helped her build her confidence.

If your toddler cries about something small and petty, bear in mind that there is probably a deeper reason for the upset, and I'll talk more about this in Chapter 9. Knowing this can help you remain calm and empathetic. Even a verbal child might not tell you what the upset is, and that's OK. You don't need to go fishing for it. They might tell you later.

Listening for the emotional cause of your child's behaviour

Being a listener is not just about listening to tears, it is also about listening to the underlying cause of our child's behaviour. When our child is acting in off-track ways we can connect with them to allow them to release the feelings behind the behaviour. The more we do this, the less our children will use their behaviour to tell us about their feelings.

When your child screams for connection

When my daughter was about 13 months old she started going through a screaming phase. It happened a lot in the mornings when I was busy getting ready to leave the house. I knew that she was feeling disconnected because I was rushing around trying to get ready, but it seemed unavoidable. I needed to make her breakfast and then get dressed so that we could go out.

I found the noise extremely irritating, it made me feel like screaming! Each time she screamed I felt more and more stressed. My usual response was just to try to meet her needs as quickly as possible. If she was screaming because the breakfast wasn't coming quickly enough, I'd grab some fruit to give her. Or if she was screaming about not being able to open her toy cupboard or get the lid off a box, I would rush over and open it for her. But the screaming continued. She seemed to be getting more and more impatient, turning into a grumpy toddler in a matter of days. I began dreading the mornings. I would usually rush to leave the house with the kitchen still a mess, and everything in chaos.

She began screaming about things that had never bothered her before; for example, running water going into her bath or people talking loudly on the train. I couldn't understand what had changed in our relationship, and why we both felt so discordant.

I had started my training to be a Hand in Hand Parenting instructor, and Patty Wipfler had explained to me that children often scream because they are afraid. It might be that the situations in which they are screaming are totally normal and innocuous but they somehow trigger memories of earlier times when our children felt very scared.

I realised that I was interpreting my daughter's screams wrongly. She wasn't really screaming because she wanted her breakfast quicker or for me to do things for her. She was actually screaming for connection.

I organised some listening time with a partner to release the stress that had been building up in me. I was able to moan, complain and scream about how irritating I found her screaming. I was amazed to find that the day after my listening session I wasn't bothered about the screaming anymore. It just seemed like a completely neutral sound.

Once I knew that there was a deeper reason beneath the screaming, I stopped rushing around. Instead, when my daughter screamed, I moved in slowly and picked her up, sometimes in the cradle position, giving her eye contact and connection. I was surprised when she arched her back and immediately started to cry, letting out all the tension in her body. For the rest of the day, every time she screamed I would do the same, pick her up slowly, being sure to connect first. She had lots of little cries spread throughout the day. In between the crying, she played happily and independently. This was an added bonus. My daughter had been clingy for so long that I had forgotten that when she was younger she did explore by herself, confident that I was close by if she needed me. I had resigned myself to the fact that babies are just clingy.

The next day she only screamed a couple of times and continued to play independently. We had a wonderful day of feeling close and connected, even as she explored while I tidied and cooked. In the evening my husband and I ate dinner for ten minutes while she played in a cardboard box on the other side of the room. Within a few more days her screaming had stopped completely.

This period of screaming really helped me to understand what it means to be present as a listener to our children, not just when they are crying but also when they ask for our attention in challenging ways. Sometimes we need to stop the rush of trying to get things done. This way of slowing down to connect was something I really had to relearn.

Slow down to listen

In the rush of our busy lives, this deep, mindful presence doesn't always come easily, especially when our own feelings get in the way. But this is what our children need in order to feel safe to show us their feelings.

It's rather like if an upset friend came to tea and all our attention was focused on being busy and distracted, rushing around the place intent on making the tea and getting biscuits but not actually listening to what they are telling us. If we sit and listen carefully, focusing on them, asking if they're OK, our presence will allow them to open up, and perhaps cry.

It's all about finding that moment after your child does something off-track that signals to us that they need connection. We can move in closely and just be there. Perhaps they will laugh – perhaps they'll cry. But it's that moment in between an emotional upset and our response which is where real connection happens.

Staylistening with more than one child

It isn't always possible to staylisten with our children. If we have one child, there may be times when we actually do need to leave the house immediately and don't have the time to wait until our child feels good. We may also struggle if we have several children. We could be listening to one child, and then another child becomes upset or starts behaving in off-track ways, as they notice our attention deeply focused on our other child. In these situations we need to make sure that everyone is safe and nothing is getting damaged. We might need to prioritise who needs our listening or attention first. If it's not possible to listen, we can gently tell our child, 'I'm sorry, but your brother/sister needs me right now, I can't listen. But I'm right here.'

Even if we can't fully listen to all our children's emotional upsets all of the time, we can still acknowledge their feelings and let them know that we're there for them.

Listening to ourselves

Our child's crying and behaviour triggers strong feelings in us: of helplessness, concern, anger or irritation. It doesn't mean that we're not a good parent. Our feelings are rooted in implicit memories that relate to how our own parents reacted to our tears and our behaviour when we were young. As we try to respond calmly, and work out ways to set limits effectively, we are also being hit by our own childhood memories of what our parents may have done at similar moments.[4] That's a lot of mental chatter to contend with.

It can be very hard to listen, even when we want to, because the majority of us simply do not have any childhood memories of being listened to until we were at the end of a big cry or being responded to gently when we misbehaved.

That's why the most important thing we can do is to be listened to ourselves. Sometimes, just talking about what irritates us about our child's behaviour, or why we find it so hard to listen to their tears and tantrums, can make these feelings vanish like magic.

Listening partnerships can provide us with the model that

we didn't receive as a child – to be listened to by someone who doesn't give advice or try to resolve our situation. Experiencing the power of listening first-hand helps us to recover our own natural instinct to listen.

Close friends and family can be good listeners too. We can laugh, cry and share experiences to ease the burden of the hard work we do as parents. But because in our culture we are stuck in patterns of trying to resolve the situation, give advice or tell our own stories, conversations with our loved ones can also divert us away from our feelings. Friends and family are so emotionally invested in wanting us to feel better as quickly as possible that they might not listen in the way that guides us through our feelings and out the other side.

Learning how to listen takes some practice, but once we have grasped it we can be a good model for those around us.

Nurturing our inner listener

It's important that we take time to nurture ourselves through listening partnerships or any other activity that helps us to feel good and bring us closer to our emotions. Physical exercise, having a massage or watching a weepy film can all help.

It can be a struggle to find me-time. When we're trying to be the perfect parent (as if there were such a thing), we often forget to take care of ourselves. This is actually just as important as taking care of our children. If we feel good, it helps them to feel good too, because of the mirror neurons that reflect our moods in each other's brain.

Some of the nurturing activities that you choose might be ones that bring you closer to your emotions. Yoga and medita-tion helped me to get out of my thinking mind and into my feeling body. I often found that when I practised yoga my emo-tions would rise to the surface, and then I would release them later with my husband or while writing. Now I have listening partnerships in the evening, and I notice the feelings coming up to be released that have been simmering during the day.

When listening doesn't come easily

If you find that you are not being the parent you want to be, it's not a sign of inadequacy, it's probably a sign that you are stressed, exhausted or overwhelmed. Perhaps there's a lot going on in your life that appears more challenging because of difficult experiences from the past. The first step is to acknowledge that you are a good parent and that you can work out what you need to make the tough job of parenting a little easier. The next step is to take practical steps to fill your own emotional cup so that it's easier to give to your child.

I learnt the Hand in Hand Parenting approach when my daughter was young, and I felt supported to be the parent I wanted to be. Just after I began writing this book my grandmother died. I had been close to her and felt devastated. I was exhausted, and suddenly the simplest things, like getting my daughter's breakfast in the morning, or even getting off the sofa, seemed incredibly hard work. I began feeling very stressed. I was snappy and shouted at my daughter. Although I was able to meet all her basic needs, there was a lot less fun and laughter in our house for a few months.

This experience reminded me that although I felt terrible and guilty about my parenting, I was still trying my best. Although at the time I couldn't do any better, I could work out what I needed to do to nurture myself so that I could slowly improve my state of well-being and work out how to get our lives back on track.

I arranged for listening partnerships each day, and the initial heavy cloud shifted as I had time to talk about my grandmother and to cry. It was useful to have this space for my feelings in a much deeper way than I would do in normal conversation. Sometimes, just talking for ten minutes about how I felt gave me the strength to get off the sofa and start my day.

After eight months things were much better, but I still wasn't the fun, playful parent I'd been before my grandmother died. No matter how much time I got for myself, it never seemed like enough, and I just couldn't enjoy being in the moment with my daughter.

Breathing through feelings

I then went to a weekend retreat for transformational breathing. When I told my daughter I wouldn't be at home for a couple of nights, she was upset. I listened to her feelings, but I still felt guilty being away from her. She had been clingy, even though I was spending a lot of time with her, and I sensed that it was because I wasn't able to fully engage with her. She needed more from me than I could give.

During the workshop my grief came to the surface, and I was able to breathe through the feelings, cry a lot and let them go. Around the room, people were laughing, or crying, or shouting in a supportive safe space where all feelings were allowed. We all finished the workshop full of joy and re-energised to return to our lives.

After the workshop I felt completely transformed. I came home full of energy and love for my daughter. I had recovered a sense of being present in the moment, and I was able to play, run and laugh again. I noticed that now, when uncomfortable emotions arose inside me, or I felt stressed or was losing patience, I simply reminded myself to be present in the moment and relax. I still felt all of my emotions fully, even more deeply than before. What had changed was that I was now able to let them go.

Nothing had been wrong with me. I'd just found parenting hard because of my upset feelings. After that, I introduced a regular breathing session into my morning routine, as well as having listening time every evening. I found a routine that worked to nurture myself and which gave me the energy to be the parent I wanted to be.

That's what worked for me. I invite you to find whatever it is in life you need to nurture your body, mind and soul. Being kind to yourself always benefits your children.

Your own listening time is essential

One of the parents I was consulting with told me about how she would often shout at her kids, give them long lectures when they were upset or acting off-track and wouldn't always listen to their feelings, even though she rationally knew of the benefits. When I asked her about her own childhood experiences she told me about her violent, aggressive father and it became obvious that her difficulties weren't because of some kind of shortcoming in herself but because her childhood had been difficult.

Once she started telling her stories during listening time, and making space in her life to nurture herself while trying not to beat herself up about her 'failings' as a parent, she found it much more easy to listen to her children's upsets.

We can use listening partnerships to work through our feelings and to enable us to feel better about our parenting, as well as to be emotionally lighter and with less emotional baggage. This will give us more joyful connected time with our children so that they will start feeling better too.

Listening to our children does take time and energy, but it's a valuable investment. When we feel able to handle our children's big emotions, parenting is easier because we're not dealing with their challenging behaviour. Our children are less full of feelings and more cooperative.

When should you start?

Take the first step to listening to your child through a full cry at home when you've got plenty of time. When your baby cries and you've been through your checklist of needs, or if your toddler starts a tantrum because he has the wrong colour cup, for example, just listen and allow him to cry until he is ready to stop. Stay close and remain empathetic. Arrange for some listening time for yourself afterwards to refill your cup.

When we begin listening, our children might start to cry more easily, sensing that we are now available to listen. Take it slowly and always notice how you are feeling. Be sure to nurture yourself afterwards, whether it's having a long, relaxing bath or some listening time when your child is in bed, or a walk in the countryside if you have a babysitter. Remember that your feelings and well-being are just as important as your child's.

Start to notice the difference in your child. Notice the little and big ways they grow in confidence or become more relaxed and cooperative. You'll probably get more cuddles too. Begin to see the healing power of tears in action.

Case Study: Alice

'My daughter fell off her bike and hurt her arm. It was a small graze, but she started crying a lot. My husband tried to distract her by talking a lot to her, asking where she felt the pain, checking and telling her that it wasn't that bad. She cried for a while, and then actually fell asleep. After ten minutes she woke up, and was like new. She looked at the wound, and smiled and was fine. Afterwards we got home, and I told her that I needed to clean the wound. She started crying again, so I waited until she had finished before

I cleaned it. By then she was happy and didn't mind me doing it.

'She was happy afterwards and actually seemed in a better mood than before she got hurt: really peaceful and relaxed. I think that the physical hurt had triggered some emotions too, and once she had our attention she knew she could let them go, and feel better.'

The following story shows how, when we struggle to listen to our child's upsets, listening time can really help.

Case Study: Julie

'I'm not always able to listen to my son's crying. I notice that I'm most able to listen when I feel good myself, about the way my life is going and when all my needs are being met, and if I'd had the chance to do something for myself. Listening time is also essential for me. If I haven't had listening time for a while, when my son starts crying I don't feel in control of my reactions. I'll start telling him things like "Stop it!" or "It's not fair what you're doing to me!", or I'll lecture him and reason with him, saying things like, "I've been doing everything you wanted the whole day."

'It's like I'm trying to get my needs met by expecting my son to behave in a certain way. I know it doesn't really work like that but I can't seem to stop the words coming out of my mouth. When I'm feeling better myself, usually after listening time, then I'm more able to just offer empathy, keep quiet and just listen.'

EXERCISE: Reflection – listening and being listened to

1   What keeps you calm and nourished? Yoga, a day at the spa or a massage? Set aside a regular time each day/week to have some regular 'me' time.

2   How did the adults around you respond to your tears when you were a child?

3   Do you know anyone who is particularly good at listening? What makes them a good listener?

4   Who could listen to you? A friend, colleague or acquaintance that you know who is a good listener?

5   Write down or talk to a listener about all the thoughts that run through your head when your child is crying. If you are the listening partner, encourage your partner to express all their thoughts without censorship.

EXERCISE: Connect

You can visit handinhandparenting.org to discover parents local to you who are practising Hand in Hand Parenting, or those you can connect with throughout the UK or worldwide via telephone or Skype.

EXERCISE: Fill your cup

Ask a partner or friend if they would like to exchange special time with you. Set a timer for 10–15 minutes and do something you love with someone paying warm attention to you. Then do the same for them.

CHAPTER 3

The Power of Attention – Why We Should Give Our Children What They Seek

•

'I'm always amazed when adults say that children "just did that to get attention". Naturally children who need attention will do all kinds of things to get it. Why not just give it to them?'

Larry J. Cohen,
psychologist and parenting expert

Our children need attention

Our children grow and thrive on attention. Research shows that giving our children focused attention literally helps them to build their brains.[1] A game of peek-a-boo, or the back and forth of talking with a baby, are not just wonderful ways to connect; all the little interactions we have with our children on a day-to-day basis are an essential part of their brain development.

As any parent knows, young children seem to want an almost infinite amount of attention, which can at times seem impossible to give amidst our busy lives. Children's brains are hardwired to seek connection with us. In our child's brain the limbic system is like a radar: constantly scanning and searching for someone to connect to. When children feel connected, their pre-frontal cortex works well, they can listen to us and use logic and reason – and their behaviour stays on-track.

When children feel disconnected or they experience upset feelings, their pre-frontal cortex can't work as well, so their behaviour starts to go off-track, and they may start seeking ways to release their feelings through laughter or tears.

The Hand in Hand Parenting tools of special time and play-listening are ways of giving children the quality attention they need to soak up to feel connected to us. This sense of connection allows them to feel safe enough to cry and release their feelings when they need to, instead of bottling up their emotions. If we are able to use the listening tools regularly, our child's cup will be full and we will find that he or she doesn't actually need our complete attention 100 per cent of the time, and that they actually enjoy oscillating between time spent interacting closely with us and time spent playing more independently.

When my daughter was nine months old, I would often do special time with her first thing in the morning. I would feel a bit silly crawling around the floor, following her lead while she went off exploring. She wouldn't look at me and hardly even seemed to notice that I was there. Then I thought to myself that of course she did notice I was there, because if I wasn't doing special time with her she wouldn't be exploring by herself, she would be clinging to me, wanting to be picked up. Often, when special time finished, and I started tidying up the kitchen or pre-paring lunch, she would continue to explore. Now that she felt that deep sense of connection to me, she could be independent.

We still try to do special time most days, and I still see that increased sense of independence in her afterwards. This con-centrated attention has a timeless quality to it. It's internalised by our children and so the connection is still there, long after special time is over.

In his book *Parenting From the Inside Out*, Dan Siegel explains how, through regular quality moments of interaction with us, our children internalise a sense of us as a safe base from which they can go out and explore the world beyond their parent. The world can range from across the room for a young baby to a teenager going to a sleepover. Whatever steps your child takes away from you, confidence and independence start with a strong connection.

The benefits of unconditional attention

As well as giving our children regular doses of special time, and bringing playlistening into our family life, we also need to be there when they are experiencing upset feelings or behaving in demanding ways, so that we can help them to release their feelings and their behaviour can get back on-track.

This is where our conventional methods of parenting actually make it much harder than it needs to be. Many conventional methods use the threat or actual withdrawal of attention as a way of controlling behaviour. It can start with the 'cry it out' method used to 'train' babies to sleep on their own by ignoring their cries. Then there is 'time out', where a child is separated from the rest of the family, albeit usually for a short period of time. One commonly held parenting philosophy is that we should 'praise the good and ignore the bad' by withdrawing attention, at least for minor misbehaviour. When children cry or tantrum we are often advised to just ignore them because this can make the crying or tantrumming stop more quickly.

On the surface, these methods can appear to work. A baby stops crying at night and learns it won't be responded to. A child tries to be good, because they want to get rewarded or they want to avoid time out. A toddler stops tantrumming when we don't pay attention to them. But underneath the surface, the feelings that caused the upset or difficult behaviour are still there.

In the long run these methods make behaviour worse, because on top of the initial upset feelings a child now feels disconnected because the parent didn't listen to them.

Sooner or later they'll start acting off-track or start to cry again, signalling that they need our help. Eventually, a child might give up trying to get our attention and become withdrawn. Inside every moody, distant teenager there's a hurt child that wanted to be listened to, and deep down still wants to be listened to even if it appears otherwise.

Whatever parenting methods we've tried, we can always begin to listen and help our child to release the feelings they've been carrying. As soon as we start listening we'll see the benefits as they become peaceful and at ease, flexible and cooperative.

Paying attention to tears

You might have noticed that if your child falls down in the playground, sometimes she doesn't cry immediately but will look around to see you before she starts crying. We could assume that if our children need our attention before they cry, they must simply be attention-seeking. You might also have noticed that if your child is upset, giving her a lot of attention makes the crying go on for longer.

Common parenting wisdom suggests that we shouldn't give too much attention to upsets. If your toddler falls over and bashes her knees while you are walking along you might pull her back up and say, 'Whoops – you're OK', then keep walking. We may have a conscious or unconscious tendency to make light of the situation, to not draw too much attention to it.

Imagine when we lived as early humans and needed to be wary of wild animals. If a baby started crying they could alert animals to its presence. If they were by themselves, it would leave them very vulnerable. Crying is a healthy physiological process, but in some situations, if a baby sensed danger and isn't feeling connected to a human they feel safe with, they wouldn't cry. Parents often notice that if their babies or children have a fright or get hurt they don't cry immediately but wait until their parent is close to them, giving them connection.

I can remember when my daughter was six weeks old, crying in her pram, I had to leave the house, and I hadn't mastered how to tie my wrap sling yet. When we got into the hallway she heard voices and immediately stopped crying. She instinctively sensed that it might not be safe to cry.

Children actually need an extra big dose of attention from us when they are crying or upset, or behaving in off-track ways that indicate there are some feelings beneath the surface. It's how we tell them that it's safe to express themselves and that we're available to listen. When we can give them that attention, and accept that they are not being 'bad', but are good children experiencing hard feelings, we can then help them to let go of those feelings so that they no longer need to demonstrate them through their behaviour.

I remember on more than one occasion as a child when I felt upset and someone asked me if I was all right. Suddenly, all the upset that I'd be holding in would well up and I would start to cry. Having someone's attention gives us the safety to actually feel our feelings and let them out. It's like that person is saying, 'It's OK – I'm here to listen and I can accept all your feelings.' We feel more sadness in the moment, but after a good cry we feel better.

You might notice that giving your child attention and eye contact, and speaking gently and kindly, can make them cry more. Offering love, warmth and support feels instinctive and yet, sometimes, we can find ourselves unconsciously starting to withdraw attention because we don't want our children to be upset. We rush away after the fall, or the situation that triggered the upset, without staying in the moment with our child.

If we become aware of our unconscious urge to do this, we can start to recognise the times when we can choose to staylisten instead. We can be there in the moment, shining our attention on our children, and allowing them to fully feel and release their emotions.

One morning when I was out, a friend came round with her dog, Mickey. At the time my daughter was in her bedroom and didn't hear the dog come in. He padded over to her open door and peeked in. She immediately left and went into the living room, then she started pulling her books and puzzles off the coffee table and throwing them onto the floor. My husband sensed something was wrong and concluded that she must have got a fright when Mickey appeared. So he picked her up and asked, 'Did Mickey give you a fright?' She burst into tears, and cried for a few minutes.

That extra dose of attention allowed her to release the fright rather than internalising it. I was really happy that my husband saw her behaviour not as something naughty but as an indication that she was upset. He was able to step in and give her the attention she needed to release the fear, stopping the behaviour in a completely gentle and loving way. Later, when I got back, we all went out for a walk and, as we were getting ready, my daughter gave Mickey a little stroke. Perhaps she wouldn't have felt safe to stroke him if she was still upset. The fear was gone and they were becoming friends.

Introducing setting limits, with attention

There is a common misconception that we cannot be firm with behaviour when we are solely focused on connection and being warm and close with our child. But the Hand in Hand Parenting listening tool of setting limits allows us to stop off-track behaviour in a way that actually builds closeness and connection.

When our child is doing something unacceptable, if we notice they are off-track and are about to throw a toy or hit their sibling, for example, we can move in close and stop the behaviour, giving them lots of eye contact and gently saying, as we bring a hand to their hand, 'I can't let you throw the toy', or 'I can't let you hit your brother'. We might find that our child naturally starts to release the feelings that were behind the behaviour. They might start laughing and wriggling out of our arms to try to throw or hit, or they might start crying or tantrumming.

We can continue to be playful while making sure that they don't repeat the behaviour. If they're in a giggly mood, we can try playlistening with them, doing whatever it takes to get the giggles going, while playfully and warmly ensuring that they don't continue with the off-track behaviour. Perhaps we might chase them around the room or gently take their hand repeatedly away from their brother with a warm smile on our face. In this way we encourage the behaviour in a playful context that keeps everyone safe. By doing so we allow our child to express their feelings through play so that they feel listened to. A good dose of play and laughter will often help them to feel connected again so their behaviour gets back on track.

It might be that they start to cry and tantrum when we set a limit. In which case we can simply staylisten with them. We give them the attention they need in whatever form they ask for. Staying with them when they have difficult feelings gives them a big dose of unconditional love and the knowledge that we will be there for them whatever they are going through. Our children's trust in us deepens as they learn that we won't withdraw attention when they are going through a challenging time. Afterwards, parenting will be easier, because we'll be closer and they will harbour fewer difficult feelings.

The attention cure

Giving our child attention is the cure for almost all of his or her difficulties, and if we start making it our intention not to withdraw our attention, our children will be able to be their natural cooperative selves.

The Hand in Hand Parenting tools are like a set of juggling balls. We'll often find that we use one and then move on to the next throughout our time with our children. I try to give my daughter regular special time and sprinkle playlistening throughout the day whenever I can. Then there will be times when she's acting a bit off-track and I might set a limit. It might be that I tell her I need to finish tidying the kitchen before we play. It's not that I will ignore her and withdraw my attention and finish tidying the kitchen, but I will listen to her feelings of upset, give her a hug and listen while gently holding the limit, telling her that I need to go and tidy up. Once she's released her feelings, she is usually happy to play independently, because the fear that stood in her way has gone.

Giving attention to ourselves

There is one time when we should withdraw our attention and that's when we feel that we're beginning to struggle to control our own emotions. Our children sense when we fake it, so it's always good to be honest about how much we are able to give. If we feel that it's an effort to stay compassionate and empathetic, while constantly trying to suppress feelings of frustration or anger, we need to step away and take some time for ourselves to calm down: going into the bathroom and taking a few deep breaths is a good emergency measure. We then need to make sure that we set aside some time to give attention to ourselves. That's why we need to include the listening partnership tool within our set of juggling balls.

After we've been using the listening tools for a while, we'll begin to see that there's always one that works. We can ask ourselves: what sort of attention does my child need? What sort of attention do I need? When we are struggling with something in our families, often one of the problems is that we are overworked and overtired. If we can take some time to pay attention to ourselves, we can begin to think more clearly about what to do.

Our children want to be good, loving and cooperative, but sometimes their feelings get in the way. Adults are no different! We can see this in our own parenting. Every day we try to do our best, but we sometimes catch ourselves saying or doing things we wish we hadn't. We can't always be the parents we want to be. We all need attention to release our feelings and become a better mother, just like our children need attention to be their natural, good, loving selves.

We can only give as much as we've received ourselves. Giving attention, even when our child is crying or behaving in challenging ways, isn't always easy and it takes practise. You might notice yourself thinking: *I'm not going to give you attention if you act like this!* or *This tantrum has been going on far too long.* These thoughts are really a sign that we need some attention for ourselves in order to have patience for our child. When we're getting frustrated or impatient with our child's upset we have our own upset child inside us who's thinking: *Hey, I didn't get attention when I tantrummed as a child! Why should I give attention to you?*

The kind of deep attention we're trying to give is something we rarely experienced as children. Our parents did their best, and they loved us deeply, but in their generation little was understood about the deep emotional connection children need. They hadn't received that level of attention either.

Connecting deeply with other human beings is our natural state. Being with our children, laughing with them, playing with them and simply enjoying their company is one of the greatest joys we will ever experience, but it gets interrupted by our own sense of hurt and lack, our implicit memories of what we didn't get when we were young. We also have a lot of responsibilities and stresses in our present lives that make it hard to give our children the attention they need. This is why it's so important that we find ways to nurture ourselves. Having regular listening time helps us to make up for some of this attention deficit. We then get a chance to release our feelings about our tantrumming or off-track child, or simply to talk about why it's so hard to provide the almost infinite amount of attention that our child seems to need.

The kind of listening that we receive in listening partnerships is something that we probably have never experienced before: someone who is there simply to listen, to pay attention to us and to hold in their minds that we are a good person, whatever challenges we are going through. Our friends love us, but conversation is often a chance to give advice or compare similar stories. We need to soak up the deep attention we get in listening partnerships just as much as our children do when we use the listening tools with them.

This 'attention medicine' translates directly into being more available for our children. I find that there is a direct correlation between the amount of listening time I've had and my ability to give high-quality attention to my daughter. It fills me with energy, patience and also creativity. If I've done some listening time recently I often find I can easily think of things to make my daughter laugh. I'm also more deeply attuned to her so that I can sense the moments when I need to connect with her so that she can cry.

If you find yourself struggling with giving your child the attention they need, it's not anything that's lacking in yourself, but just an indication that you need some attention for yourself. I go into greater detail about listening partnerships in Chapter 4.

My story – clearing the way to giving attention

When my daughter was one year old, she went through a stage where she started biting me every day. It often happened if I was holding her while trying to write a quick email, or distractedly looking for an item of clothing in the wardrobe. It was clear she was asking me for attention as it almost always happened when I was busy doing something else. It was a surprise that this was happening since I'd been working hard on being connected to her. Why was she suddenly giving me this sign that she was feeling disconnected? Later I learnt that when we start listening to our children they grow in confidence and may start telling us about their deeper feelings and upsets.

Of course, it's natural that young children want a big chunk of our attention throughout the day, but why did my daughter have such a sudden reaction to me focusing on something else for a few minutes?

Aggression is often a sign that our children are fearful,[2] and those small moments of my busy preoccupation were triggering feelings of disconnection.

I got good at intercepting the bites before they happened, but one time I didn't. She bit me really hard, and held on to my flesh for a few seconds. For a moment we just stared at each other like wild animals, as I wondered when she was going to let go.

Since I knew she needed my attention, I decided to give her some special time, even though I felt a bit irritated. I gently told her not to bite me again: then I began to think about where the fear might have come from. She was a happy, relaxed baby, but I knew that there was an underlying sense of fear that must have come from her birth. My anger disappeared when I reflected on what a hard time she'd gone through. I started crying and then was able to play with her without the underlying sense of resentment.

It was giving my daughter the attention that she needed that eventually solved her biting problem. I began to help her channel the aggression in some laughter play and we had a lot of fun as she playfully 'attacked' me with her hands while I deflected her. Many traditional parenting approaches would suggest that this kind of play encourages 'bad' behaviour, but research has shown that playful roughhousing actually reduces aggression in children.[3] I didn't allow my daughter to bite or kick or hit me, but it was a playful way to set limits. By catching the kicks or hits before they actually touched my body I remained in control and helped her to release the feelings, through laughter, behind the impulse to be aggressive.

One morning she bit me again. I didn't have time to deflect her or have a playful response. I gently said, 'Please don't bite', and she burst into tears. Before, when I had told her not to bite, it hadn't been enough to stop her. I'm sure that warming up our connection through lots of play, and channelling the aggression, allowed my daughter's feelings to come closer to the surface so that this time, when I set a limit, she was able to cry and release the feelings behind the aggression. After that she stopped biting me and never bit me again.

This was a clear example to me of how it benefits our children and improves their behaviour when we can rise above our own feelings of irritation or anger and keep coming back to give them the attention that they need, while setting firm but gentle limits on the behaviour we find unacceptable. You can read more about setting limits in Chapter 12.

Listening time can help us work on the feelings that stand in the way of giving our 'misbehaving' child attention. We can get help for the hurt child who didn't get the attention we are trying to give by talking about our own feelings. We can moan and complain about how hard it is to give our child unconditional attention. We can recall how our parents would have treated us if we 'misbehaved' in similar ways. Then we can shower our children with attention, helping them with the hurt feelings that make them feel disconnected from us, so that any negative behaviour issues become a chance to come closer together. The reward for this hard work is to see our child's true nature shining through: cooperative, loving and full of joy.

Case Study: Debbie

'I've noticed that when I've got a lot of attention to give my eight-month-old daughter, when I'm really present and fully in the moment with her, that's often when she chooses to cry. It might be that we've been playing happily together, and then immediately afterwards she'll start crying.

'On the days when I'm distracted, busy and pre-occupied, when I have a lot of emails to write or places to go, then she won't cry. She'll look away from my eyes or suck her thumb, withdrawing from me, holding in those feelings until I'm available to listen again. Becoming aware of this pattern has taught me how to pay attention, to notice when she's not giving eye contact or when she's sucking her thumb. I then try to slow down and spend time with her playing peek-a-boo to get her laughing or smiling, to notice these little disconnected moments and bring us back to connection.'

This next story shows that when we find it hard to give attention in the present it can be because of our own childhood experiences. Getting listening time and having our story heard means that we can become the parent we want to be.

Case Study: Sandra

'When my daughter was three I began to feel really tired. I felt like our days together were much harder than they used to be. She would want to talk all day and I found it exhausting answering all her questions and replying to everything she said. If I was slow to answer her, she would always repeat herself, sounding whiny and impatient, which made me feel even worse. When I reflected on it during listening time, I realised that it had started when she was about two and a half and she had suddenly started talking a lot. Before that she'd had less than 20 words.

'My listening partner asked what it was like for me when I was the same age. I remembered my mum saying that when I was two she had been pregnant with my sister, and I had wanted to talk a lot but she was a quiet person and didn't want to talk much. With my listening partner I was able to cry and let go of some of the upset about my mum not listening to me. Afterwards, I had more attention for my daughter, and I could enjoy her company more and empathise with her need to talk and connect with me.'

EXERCISE: Reflection – when you find giving attention difficult

1   What feelings come up for you when your child wants your attention and you don't have much to give? Say all the frustrated, angry thoughts that come to you. Let them out in a listening partnership so that they don't get in the way of your parenting.

2   Who gave you attention as a child? Do you remember craving more? Who do you wish gave you more attention?

EXERCISE: Try this – discover how listening time affects special time

1   Give your child some special time, noticing how you feel about giving attention. Is it easy, or an effort?

2   Later, in a listening partnership, reflect on how it was for you, the thoughts and feelings that were running through your head while you were giving special time. Did the experience remind you of anything from your own childhood?

3   Do another special time. Was it easier after being able to process your own feelings?

CHAPTER 4

Listening Partnerships – Putting on Your Own Oxygen Mask First

•

'Too often we underestimate the power
of a touch, a smile, a kind word, a listening
ear, an honest compliment, or the smallest act
of caring, all of which have the potential
to turn a life around.'

Leo Buscaglia,
author and motivational speaker

This book shares a revolutionary way of parenting: that if we simply create the safety and connection our children need to release their feelings they will be their natural, good, cooperative selves and parenting will be easier and more full of joy. There's one thing that stands in our way, and that's us and our own feelings. If you've started listening to your children's upsets, playing or doing special time with them, you'll notice that it's really hard when you're not feeling good yourself. Sometimes laughing with our kids or giving them one-to-one attention builds our sense of connection too, so we actually feel better. But at other times, we need something more; we need an adult to listen to us. As I explained in Chapter 1, using the illustration of flying safety instructions, we need to put on our own metaphorical oxygen mask by obtaining our personal emotional support before we can listen effectively to our child.

The healing power of tears starts with us. We didn't get this kind of listening as children so we have some catching up to do. Listening partnerships offer us the chance to experience the same quality of listening that we are learning to give our children. It becomes a lot easier to listen deeply to them when we understand first-hand what that really means.

I remember feeling very isolated when I first learnt about the healing power of tears. None of the other parents around me seemed to know about it, apart from a baby-massage teacher who'd come to my house to teach me. I felt confused. How could I possibly parent in this way when it seemed completely different from the approach of almost every other parent I knew?

When I started my first listening partnership, it was such a relief to be able to talk to someone who was going through a similar process. I realised that part of the confusion I felt stemmed from my own history with crying. When I could share this with someone else I felt less isolated and confused.

Just like our children, we need to feel well connected to others in order to think effectively and to function well.[1] This is why we need support, especially for something as emotionally complex as parenting. Human connection is essential for adults as well as children.

We may already have close friends or family members that are good listeners and with whom we feel comfortable talking about our problems. We might spend time laughing with our loved ones, or even crying, and that's great. During everyday conversation, however, there isn't always the time to fully explore our feelings. When we have conversations with people, they will often use the cultural habits of trying to reassure us or to make us feel better as quickly as possible, or they will offer solutions. Conversation is also a shared space, so when we vent frustration about our toddler not sleeping, our friend might jump in and have a moan about theirs too.

The back-and-forth of conversation doesn't often give us the time to heal.

Listening partnerships are different because they have one single purpose: to allow us a set period of uninterrupted time to recover our natural healing process. We are able to focus solely on our own internal thoughts with a supportive listener who is fully focused on us and who can help to guide us towards releasing our feelings.

How listening partnerships work

As explained earlier, in a listening partnership, two people take turns talking and listening for a set period of time. You can use a timer to keep the turns equal. Listening partnerships where both people are present are particularly powerful, but you can also do them via phone or Skype.

You could start a listening partnership with a friend or acquaintance who is a good listener. Or you can find other parents practising Hand in Hand Parenting in your area or online through Hand in Hand Parenting. You could check if there's a Hand in Hand Parenting instructor near you and take a course to learn the basics. There are also online courses provided by Hand in Hand. A course isn't essential, but they are extremely beneficial because they allow you to experience being listened to by an instructor who has had years of practice.

It's not a good idea to start your first listening partnership with your spouse. Because they are emotionally invested in the intricacies of your life, it is hard for them to act as a neutral listener. Later, you might find that you can do listening time together, or at least use some of the listening skills you have learnt when you talk to them (for more about this see Chapter 16). But in the beginning, when you are developing your skills, it's best to practise with someone outside your immediate family.

Whoever you choose as your listening partner, it's a good

idea to ask them to read this book or the listening partnerships booklet from Hand in Hand Parenting so that you can both learn how the process works and follow the same listening guidelines. You can choose to talk for any period between five minutes to an hour each; however, when you first start it's good to talk for longer time periods while you get to know each other. This helps to build up empathy and to understand your partner's life.

Allocating time to your listening partnership

Ideally, it's best to set up a weekly listening partnership of 30 minutes each way. This gives you the chance to work through minor ups and downs, and to clear the way for focusing on any deeper issues you are facing. As well as regular sessions, you can also ask for 'emergency' listening time, for those times when you are feeling stressed, exhausted or angry.

In our busy lives, where there is never enough time, starting a listening partnership can seem like just another item on our to-do list. Until you've tried it, it's hard to imagine the benefits. But the very reason that I've written this book and have learnt a whole parenting philosophy that has transformed my life is because someone listened to Patty Wipfler for fifteen minutes.

It's powerful stuff, and it's not just being listened to that has benefits. When we are listening to someone, we are focusing our attention on them so that it affects our brain in a similar way to meditation, reducing stress and increasing emotional well-being. When we are consumed by our own worries, it's also helpful to take our focus away from them for a while when we can help someone else.

Just as investing time playing and connecting with our children allows life to go more smoothly, so does investing time in exploring our own feelings. When we clear our mind of emotional debris we spend less time consumed by worries, confusion or feeling low. We can think more clearly about how to make our lives go well.

Our listening partnership is a safe space

One of the most important rules for listening partnerships is to keep everything confidential. That means not telling other people what you hear during a listening time. It also means not referring to what that person has said outside the listening time or in your own listening time. This creates a safe space, so that each person talks only about their issues when they are ready to, not because their partner decides to bring them up.

The Hand in Hand Parenting philosophy is that all children are fundamentally good, and when they have upset feelings they cannot think clearly and they therefore behave in off-track ways. Adult emotions work in exactly the same way. When we have difficulties or make mistakes it's because we are feeling stressed or upset. Often the root cause is how we have been hurt in the past; for example, if someone grew up in a household where their parents were arguing all the time, they might find they cannot handle conflict well and get really stressed and upset by it. They might respond by shouting and screaming in an angry rage or they might do the complete opposite and refuse to discuss important issues at all. This could be construed as a failing in themselves, but it's much more helpful to see it as an area of their life where they still carry hurt. Talking and releasing feelings about what happened in the past can help them move forward in their life and work out how to handle conflict more effectively.

We learn to respect each other's difficulties

When we listen to our partner we should hold in our minds that they are the best expert on their own family. We might wonder why certain areas of their life are full of difficulty when to us the solution seems obvious; however, as we listen carefully, and hear about their past and present, we'll begin to see that there are complex reasons why their life is the way it is. When we listen it should always be from a position of non-judgement. We should remember that they are a good parent, doing the best they can.

Keeping this in mind is a powerful healing mechanism in itself. When we did things wrong as children we might have been shouted at or punished. It was certainly a rare occurrence if someone understood the complex feelings behind our behaviour. Now we can receive unconditional positive regard. Our partner knows our struggles and still thinks we are a good person.

We now have a place where we can go to release the guilt and shame that we've been carrying – to know that we are still good. We can forgive ourselves for our own shortcomings as a parent. It's not that we aren't responsible for our actions; for example, if we're frequently losing our temper with our children, it is our responsibility to work out how to change. But through the listening process we understand that our off-track behaviour is a reflection of specific ways in which we've been hurt. We deserve to be kind to ourselves and to have a warm, supportive listener to tell our stories to.

We can learn what it means to unconditionally accept our own feelings, as we try to do the best we can. We can then extend this unconditional positive regard to our own children, knowing that they are deeply good and always doing their best too. Accepting our feelings, and our children's, is the first step in allowing healing to begin.

Being the speaker

When it's your turn to be listened to, you can choose to talk about anything you like. You can work through the exercises in this book or simply talk about how parenting is going. When you start a new listening partnership, telling your life story is a great way to start. As you talk, notice the feelings that come up and pause to make space for them. You might find yourself laughing, crying, yawning or even shaking as your body finds ways to naturally release stress and tension it is carrying.

As you talk, your partner will listen with warmth and pay close attention to what you are saying. It might feel a bit unusual at first. We aren't used to having this kind of attention given to us.

I remember one of the first times I was listened to. As my partner looked at me, waiting for me to speak, I immediately started crying without even knowing why. Later, I reflected that having someone there ready to listen to me triggered feelings of not being given this kind of attention when I was young. Simply having this space for ourselves allows healing to start happening.

Notice any emotions that come up about being listened to and voice them to your partner. Perhaps you will laugh with embarrassment or feel the urge to hide away or not look at your partner. You don't need to rush through your story or relate it when you're not feeling completely comfortable. It's much more beneficial to take your time to notice and feel everything that comes up for you.

You can keep returning to your life story for a number of sessions until you've finished telling it up to the present time. As you tell it, you might notice prominent events that are difficult to talk about, which you still have a lot of feelings about. It might be a good idea to write a list of them and make a mental note to return to them during another listening time. This is one of the ways that we can make our stories more coherent: by going back and telling and retelling the parts where they get difficult.

After telling your life story, a good format for regular listening partnerships is to start with what's going well, so that you focus on the positive as well as the challenging aspects of your life. You can then begin to work on present-day challenges. You might start by running through some of the minor challenges you've faced throughout the week; then you'll probably find that you focus on a larger challenge that needs more time and attention.

This format is just a guide. Our mind tends to jump around

in a stream-of-consciousness way that might not always make sense to us. Part of this process is learning how to listen to our emotional side without the logical, judging mind getting in the way and saying, 'I shouldn't say that' or suggesting that it is pointless. We should trust that our unconscious is working out what we need to say to get the healing process started.

What if I can't think of anything to say?

There may be times when you are talking and then your mind goes blank, or you forget what you wanted to say, or you feel like everything is actually fine in your life and you don't have any problems to talk about. It's funny how our mind is full of thoughts, but when someone shines their attention on us we can occasionally go blank. Sometimes in listening time it can be helpful to move the body, to shake or stretch a bit when we feel stuck in a particular emotion or we can't think what to say. Since our emotional baggage is stored in our body, this can be a powerful way to access what we are feeling, and to release it. When we listen to our partner we can invite them to do the same if it seems needed.

Linking our emotions with the past

When we focus on our present-day challenges, it can be helpful to try to trace them back to the past. To ask ourselves the question (or our listener might ask us), for example, if the current situation reminds us of something from our past.

When I first started teaching parenting workshops I got incredibly nervous. I knew my material, and the classes always went well, despite my nerves. There was nothing inherently scary about teaching, but I still felt uncomfortable. I then realised that memories from my childhood were being triggered – memories of being bullied or put down by other children, especially in situations where a teacher had praised me for good work or given me attention in front of the class. It was only when I went back to talk about these memories that I recovered my confidence.

Sometimes all we need is the warmth of a listener to allow us to find whatever feelings we need to release. But it can be challenging to undo the habits of avoiding our feelings. After years of not being fully listened to, it's as if we have doors with locks to shut away our feelings, and some are easier to open than others.

Your listener might offer you directions or questions to help you express yourself; for example, if you're having a difficult time getting your toddler dressed in the mornings, you might be trying your best to be patient and calm with them when you actually feel like shouting.

During listening time, your listener might ask you to express whatever you feel like doing or saying in those moments without censoring yourself. You can shout and scream and say everything you try your best not to say in front of your child. This will help you to release your stress about the situation, so next time your toddler is being non-cooperative in the morning you will find it easier to be calm and think up a creative solution to help her.

If your partner asks something, or suggests you do something during the listening session, it's always OK not to follow their direction. It's important to remember that it's your listening time and it's always your choice about what you talk about. Remember, however, that it's not the listening partner's role to make suggestions or to try to solve the situations you are talking about; you are the one in control of directing your listening time.

If you have taken the listening role first, when it is your turn to talk you might find that your mind tends to wander down a similar track to theirs. When this happens, you shouldn't say, 'Oh I'm concerned about my son watching too much TV as well.' If you refer back to your partner's situation, your listener might jump back into their own feelings rather than remaining a neutral listener for you. It's fine to talk about similar subjects to your partner, but you should remember not to draw parallels between your life and theirs to ensure that we keep their story confidential.

Listening Partnerships – the basics

1 Always set a timer to keep the turns equal.
2 Keep everything confidential. Don't refer to it outside the listening partnership, even to the person you were listening to.

When you are the listener

1 Listen without interrupting, trying to fix or tell your own story.
2 Keep in mind that the person you are listening to is fundamentally good and is the best expert on their own life.
3 Ask questions or offer empathy and encouragement if you sense it will help the person get deeper into their feelings.

When you are the speaker

1 Follow the natural flow of the thoughts in your mind.
2 Feel free to accept or reject the directions your listener might give you – it's your listening time.

Being the listener

Listening is a natural instinct that we can all uncover. As we practise, we'll learn how to intuitively help our partner to release their feelings. There is an art to it that develops over time, but even in the beginning just being there is powerful. We are offering something amazing that our partner might never have experienced before: someone who is giving them a safe space to explore their feelings.

We should listen with warmth, remembering that our partner is a good person and an expert on their family life. We should refrain from giving advice, interrupting or telling our own stories. We might notice that thoughts pop up into our minds like,

Oh, that happened to me, or *Oh, I'm worried about my son starting pre-school too!* We should just let these thoughts pass by and keep our attention on our partner.

Our main job is simply to listen to our partner, to follow their train of thought without interrupting. At first it can seem strange and unusual to listen to someone without saying much. As time goes on you'll learn just how powerful it is to simply be there, thinking well of your partner and showing an interest in their story.

Most of our time will be spent listening. If our partner is telling their stories, and releasing their emotions through laughing and crying, yawning or shaking, then all we need to do is just keep listening. If they're talking but no feelings are being released, we can also help our partner to let their natural healing process flow.

If your partner is worried about their inadequacies as a parent, for example, it can help if you reassure them that they are a good parent and that you can see that they're doing their best. They might laugh or cry hearing these words as they start to understand that it's true. They can now let go of old feelings about not being good enough. They'll start to believe the truth of our words and their confidence will grow.

There may be times like this when your partner is getting bogged down in feelings that aren't ultimately true; for example, if they think they're not a good parent but we can see they are actually doing a really good job. It's beneficial if we can remind them of the ultimate truth of things; for example, if a parent is having a difficult time with a child and feels that their relationship is frayed, we could remind them that their child loves them. Or we could ask them to recall a moment when they felt really close to their child. This counteracts the present difficulty and helps them to release their feelings. When upset isn't clouding their mind, they can work out a way to rebuild closeness.

If your partner seems to hesitate, or feel unsure about saying something, you can remind them that they are free to say whatever they like. Perhaps tell them that you won't judge them. Or you could ask them what they are thinking.

Prompts for listening

Questions can help your partner to get back to the early origins of their problem and release their feelings. Here are a few examples of possible questions.

- 'Can you say a bit more about that?'
- 'When did this begin?'
- 'When did you first feel this way?'
- 'What was the first time you remember this happening to you?'
- 'What does this remind you of?'
- 'Who does he/she remind you of?'
- 'Was there ever a time when it wasn't this way?'
  (From the Listening Partnerships for Parents *booklet by Patty Wipfler.)*

These questions are just suggestions. You might think of your own along similar lines. As you gain listening experience, you will find that you begin to work out the kind of directions that will help your partner get to their feelings. As you listen to your partner, you might find that something pops into your mind that you think might help. If you do say something, or ask a question, it should arise naturally, rather than because you feel that you should say something. I have always found that if nothing pops into my head to say, I should just focus on listening and not try to force it.

You might also find that you feel like laughing or crying along with your partner. It's OK to laugh along with them or to let out a few tears if you feel moved. The important thing is not to make your partner's listening time more about your emotions, so don't laugh longer or louder than they do, and don't let your tears get in the way of listening. It's important that we keep focusing on their emotions rather than our own.

As you listen to your partner, you might find your own issues simmering in the background. Perhaps you also have a difficult relationship with your father, or your toddler is also being aggressive. You should try to let these thoughts go, and return to listening. If this happens, it's an indication that at some point you need some listening time on that subject too.

Ending the turn

After each person finishes their turn we ask an 'attention out' question. Questions like these take our partner's attention away from their emotions and back to the present moment so that they can listen to us or return to their daily life. We might ask our partner to describe the view out of the window, for example, or to explain how to get to the nearest shop from their house.

Listening relationships

When we begin our listening partnership we might find that we instantly like our partner and feel that we fit well together. Sometimes, however, it can take longer to feel completely comfortable with someone. Sharing our private lives can release all kinds of feelings in us. It's worth giving each listening partnership a chance, but it's also important to know that it's OK to back out if it's not working after a while. We need to trust the other person and feel safe enough to share with them.

Like any relationship in our life, we need to nurture our listening partners, to show them that we value and appreciate them. If my partner says something in a session that has really helped me get to my feelings, I'll often tell them afterwards and say thank you. If a particular listening session completely turned my day around, I might drop my listening partner a quick email to let them know how much they helped me.

When we share this kind of deep listening with someone, we grow to feel love for them. They might live next door to us or thousands of miles away, but we gain a powerful strength from supporting each other.

IMPORTANT NOTE: There may be times when listening partnerships bring up strong feelings in us that can be hard to cope with. Listening partnerships should be a positive, healing experience that help us to live our lives with our children with more joy. If at any time you find yourself overwhelmed by feelings, or you are struggling to cope and are not experiencing the benefits, it is advisable to seek advice from your GP or from a professional counsellor.

Case Study: Ali

'I began to get really irritated by my son's eating habits. He always wanted to snack, and I was worried he was eating too much. I also found the way he ate quite disgusting, making really loud smacking sounds and dropping crumbs everywhere. When I talked about it in my listening time, my listening partner asked me if there was anyone I could recall who ate like that. A memory flashed into my head of sitting at the dining-room table with my dad. At the dinner table there would often be a lot of conflict and arguments between my parents. At other times there would be silence and heavy tension in the air. It was amazing the way something like my son's eating had this whole story attached to it that had nothing to do with the present.

'After talking with my listening partner I started being much more relaxed about my son's eating. My head was clearer to work out ways to bring more healthy food into the house. I could also even go to McDonald's with my son for special time and treat him without feeling uptight and worried!'

EXERCISE: Reflection – think about listening and talking

1   How is parenting going? What are the minor challenges you are dealing with at the moment?

2a What are the major challenges you have in your life right now? What are the things you wish were better? Do you have a big decision you need to make?

2b Do the feelings that these challenges evoke remind you of anything that's happened in the past?

2c If there are certain people that you are struggling with in your life right now, do they remind you of anyone from your past?

3   What can you take off your to-do list, or at least put aside for a while?

4   Imagine a day off from parenting – what would you do?

CHAPTER 5

Raisin Distraction – How We Inadvertently Stop Tears

•

'The walls we build around us to keep sadness out
also keep out the joy.'

Jim Rohn, American entrepreneur,
author and motivational speaker

One day I was in the supermarket with my daughter. There was a little trolley that she was enjoying pushing around. When it was time to go, I knelt down and gently told her that we had to put the trolley back. She started to cry and I stayed there listening to her, thinking that she would stop after a moment or two and then we could leave. Then a woman swooped in and popped a raisin into her mouth. She stopped crying instantly. On the surface it looked as if the problem had been solved, and we left the shop without any more tears.

One raisin isn't going to hurt, but over time, if we continually stop our children's tears with distraction or food, they will begin to get the same message that most of us received as children: that tears aren't welcome, that when we experience uncomfortable feelings we should look for something to stop them, rather than simply feel them and then let them go.

When children grow older, they might develop the habits that many of us have of reaching for something to distract ourselves from strong emotions, such as coffee or ice cream as a pick-me-up, or alcohol at the end of the day. They wouldn't get to experience the greater sense of well-being that comes from being able to process their feelings in a healthy way.

I've subsequently written a list of the things that people have done to cheer my daughter up in public when she's been crying. From a bag of sweets, to a packet of stickers, to one time when she got her big winter boots stuck in a trolley in an electronics shop and the shop assistant gave her a Duracell bunny.

A quick-fix for feelings?

Fixing problems with food, distraction or material objects is a short-term solution. It looks as if it works because the tears stop, but in the long run it makes parenting much harder than it needs to be. All the feelings that didn't get released start building up and manifest as emotional or behavioural difficulties. Children might also become increasingly demanding as they get into habits of asking for sweet foods, TV or constant entertainment as a means to distract themselves from their feelings.

Every time we are able to listen to our children's feelings, we empty their 'emotional backpack' so that they're less likely to tell us how they feel through off-track behaviour. Listening prevents challenging behaviour before it happens.

The list I compiled contained some obvious examples of times when adults were trying to stop my daughter from crying. There are also less obvious moments in which we might be inadvertently stopping our children from crying without even being aware of it.

It's inevitable that we'll get into patterns of stopping our children's feelings because of our own upbringing and the cultural attitudes around us towards crying. We are just learning how to listen, and it takes some working out along the way. The good news is that children and adults can always catch up on their crying later. We can also bring our awareness to some of the situations in which we may be unknowingly stopping crying and choose to listen instead.

Making sense of small daily problems

When my daughter was born it took me a while to untangle when she had a need or when she just needed to cry; for example, she hated having tops pulled over her head and would always start to cry when I tried to put them on. I would rush through the moment, trying to get it over with as quickly as possible. My aim was to make sure that she would cry for the absolute minimum amount of time. I came to dread every time I had to get her dressed, because she always got upset.

I remember having a light-bulb moment when I read something Patty Wipfler had written about babies having clothes pulled over their heads. She explained that it can trigger upset and fear that possibly relates to early trauma such as birth difficulties or medical intervention. Reading Patty's words made me realise that I was uncomfortable with my daughter expressing her upset, and was trying to avoid it. Getting dressed was one of the times I had been unknowingly stopping her from crying. I suddenly realised I could do things differently.

Next time I dressed her, I showed her the clothes and told her that we needed to put them on, but I didn't do it straight away. She cried for a few moments, and then when the crying died down, I would gently tell her again that I needed to put them on. She cried a bit more, and I held her and reassured her that it would be OK and that I would keep her safe. When she stopped crying, I would move towards putting the clothes on, but if she started crying again I would stop what I was doing and just hold her.

After a while she finished crying, and I could put the clothes over her head, and she was completely relaxed and happy. I didn't need to force the clothes on against her will; I just needed to wait until she was ready. Instead of it being something I was doing to her, it became something we did together, in her own time.

The next time she didn't get upset at all. She had released all the feelings associated with having clothes pulled over her head. After that, something that I had begun to dread became something we could do without any stress or tears.

Emotional moments

You might notice that there are similar moments in your own parenting, something that brings up a lot of feelings for your baby or toddler, something that you rush through and that neither of you enjoy. We don't want to do anything against our child's will and we also feel uncomfortable with their upsets because when we were small adults weren't comfortable with ours.

We can bring what we know about crying to these situations, and reframe them as healing opportunities. We can be more conscious of what we're doing and notice if we are trying to avoid our child's crying. We can make sure that we allow space for their feelings in the way I talked about in Chapter 2.

Regarding newborns, there are lots of situations that seem strange and unusual even though they will be completely safe, everyday occurrences; for example, having a bath, nappy change, going in a car seat or having their nose or face wiped.

In some of these situations, it's unavoidable: we need to change a nappy or put our baby in the car seat. We might rush through these moments in order to keep crying to a minimum. We don't want them to have unpleasant experiences, so we try to get them over with as quickly as possible. It can seem automatic to use a toy or perhaps play some music or sing to cheer them up.

If we look closely we are probably trying to distract them from their feelings. In a sense we are tricking our child into doing something that they feel uncomfortable about by drawing their attention elsewhere.

Babies and children often attach their fears on to everyday events where there is no real threat, so that they can bring them up in an environment that feels safe.[1] It can appear that they are scared of a certain situation, but if we listen carefully we'll often find that once they get a chance to express their feelings, the fear is gone.

Staying in the moment to understand upsets

We can talk to our babies and toddlers even when they are young and non-verbal to explain what we need to do. We can show them the bath or the car seat and move towards putting them in, but then we can stop and wait if they get upset. This way we are staying in the moment, allowing them to feel what's upsetting them, rather than avoiding it. We can hold them and allow them to finish crying. We can try again when they stop crying, and then pause and listen if they start crying again. Because we aren't distracting them, they are fully aware and involved in what's happening. This builds trust and is the beginning of cooperation between you and your child.

When your baby is free of the stress and anxiety they've been carrying, these everyday moments won't seem so scary any more. Your baby will get to enjoy bath time, nappy changing and even teeth cleaning when their teeth start coming through. Even routine tasks can be full of enjoyment for our babies and toddlers, when their reactions aren't clouded by upset.

It takes time to listen to crying, and we don't always have that time, or feel in the right frame of mind to listen. We might find that we don't always notice the moments when we could be listening and allowing feelings, or we do notice them but just feel like we can't handle the feelings. That's an indication that we need to refill our own cup and do something to nurture ourselves – such as having some listening time for ourselves.

If we can listen to our baby as often as possible, it's an investment of time that pays off into the toddler years. If your baby gets to release a lot of their early fears and upsets, then there will be fewer daily struggles connected to teeth cleaning or nappy changing, because they have less of a backlog of feelings. Allowing feelings to be expressed as often as possible builds cooperation in the moment and in the future.

Time for laughter

There are times when we need to do something but our child won't cooperate although he doesn't seem upset by the situation. Connecting in a playful way allows emotions to flow through laughter; for example, when my daughter was old enough to roll and get on to all fours, she would sometimes do this while I tried to change her nappy. I tried to change her nappy like that, although it was quite awkward, then I realised that I was avoiding her feelings in another way. She was showing me that she needed to play, connect and laugh with me.

The next time, I brought some play into the situation. So, for example, I would tap her on the shoulder, and say 'Excuse me', which triggered a lot of giggles. Then after a while of doing this, she just rolled on to her back and lay there. It amazed me that even as a young baby she knew exactly what I wanted her to do, and she would cooperate when she felt connected to me. I didn't need to force her, or roll her over on to her back, or try to get serious about changing her nappy while she wriggled around trying to play. If I allowed her feelings, we could cooperate.

When she was a bit older, she went through a stage when if I suggested it was time to clean her teeth or put her pyjamas on she would immediately run away from me. She didn't do this with my husband, and so sometimes I'd just let him clean her teeth. Then I realised that this was avoidance on my part. She was bringing her feelings to me, because she sensed I was the parent who listened the most. She wanted me to help her with her feelings.

The next time I decided to take some time to listen and do some playlistening with her. I chased her, always allowing her to escape, so that she had the more powerful role. It really got her giggling, and as I watched the passing minutes on the clock, I knew that this investment of time would mean that the next night she'd probably happily get her pyjamas on without any objections, because she'd played away her feelings the previous night. If we focus on allowing feelings as much as possible, rather than stopping them, life goes much more smoothly.

The feelings behind our toddler's requests

Even with our best attempts to listen to our children's feelings, they might get into the habit of asking for things to distract themselves. TV, chocolate or crisps are things my daughter loves, but I also notice that sometimes she asks for them when it seems like something's bothering her.

One evening, for example, I had to go out at short notice. I was a bit nervous about the separation from my daughter because the next day she was starting a new playgroup. She cried when I first told her I would be out but then seemed OK with it; however, as I was walking out the door she immediately asked my husband for some sweet rice cakes and I wondered if she was still upset about me leaving.

In the mornings we almost always sit on the sofa and cuddle for five minutes before starting our day, but the next morning she wouldn't look at me or talk, except to ask to watch TV, which we rarely do if we are going out first thing. I was sure that her desire to watch TV stemmed from not feeling connected enough to show me how she was feeling, and she was trying to distract herself.

I said no, and she cried for a few minutes. When she stopped crying, I mentioned the playgroup and told her she could stay home if she wanted to, and she cried and said she really wanted to go. Then I said that if she got upset she could always go to one of the teachers and they would look after her, and she cried. Each time I said something to make the situation feel safer for her, it led to another wave of crying. She was letting go of whatever feelings were standing in her way.

After that, she was in a much happier mood. I did her hair and a hairband pinged across the room by mistake, and she giggled. I took this as an opportunity for some playlistening, and pinged it a few more times, acting exasperated by my 'mistake' while she laughed. Then she happily went off to her playgroup, and I could see visibly how letting out those nerves and sense of disconnection had helped her inner confidence to grow.

Recognising hidden upset in your child

If your toddler asks for something or to do something, there may be times when you can sense an underlying urgency or grumpiness to the request. You can slow down, move in closer and make eye contact. You can tell her that you'll get whatever she wants in a minute. If there are some underlying feelings of disconnection or upset, when you offer your connection your child might start crying and letting go of the frustration that made her feel impatient or desperate.

My daughter always waits for about 15 minutes after waking before asking for breakfast in the morning. One morning, however, she woke up and instantly complained in a whiny voice that she was hungry. The night before she had had a full dinner before bed, so I was surprised. I was just about to start making her breakfast when she started crying because of something completely unrelated. When she asked again for her breakfast I told her that I would get it in a minute, and I listened until she was happy again. She didn't ask for breakfast again but wanted to play and do special time. I realised she hadn't actually been really hungry, but just that she misinterpreted her upset feelings as hunger, and when those feelings were gone she didn't feel hungry anymore. Perhaps this misinterpretation was because when she was a young baby I didn't fully understand about the healing power of tears and would often feed her when she just needed to cry. Continuing to listen rather than rushing around getting the breakfast immediately could help us to undo that habit she'd formed of eating when she was upset.

There are times when we feel tired, stressed or busy, and we might notice that we can't seem to find the time or energy to listen to our child's upsets. It's OK to acknowledge our limitations. We can always help them recover later when we have filled our own cup again.

We can listen as much as possible, and know that every moment we create a safe space for our child's feelings we are giving a gift to them, something way beyond what we probably received as children. They'll grow up internalising this knowledge of how feelings naturally flow, so that when stress and upset occur they don't need to hold on to those feelings indefinitely, but can let them go.

Why we block our own feelings

The ways in which we inadvertently stop our children from crying are often based on the way adults around us reacted to our tears when we were small. This process begins in infancy and the toddler years when parents, teachers or other adults tried to manage our more explosive emotions. We then continue these patterns of trying to control our own emotions when we become adults. We also have a tendency to repeat this and try to control our children's emotions in similar ways.

Listening time allows us to break this cycle. We can tell the stories of how the adults reacted to our crying as children, the times when our emotions weren't fully accepted or listened to. With the presence of a warm, caring listener we can counteract those experiences by receiving the empathy we didn't get as children. We can then extend that empathy to our children and naturally move away from stopping feelings towards listening instead.

As well as telling our past stories about crying, talking about our present difficulties, and tracing them back to the past, can also make it easier to allow our children to cry. The fact that the hard times in our past are still affecting us is a sign that we didn't get to heal fully or recover at the time. We can trace back each difficulty to find the places where we didn't fully get to cry and express our upset. We can then express the emotion with a listener and create a new story, one in which our feelings didn't get stopped but were fully allowed and empathised with.

Each time we do this it becomes easier to see when our children need to cry because we have first-hand knowledge of the natural, healthy ways our emotions work. The understanding that we reach about our own emotional stories allows us to have understanding and patience for the rich and complex emotional lives of our children.

Without past stories interfering with our thinking, we can be more consciously aware in the present moment and find our deepest instinct to listen. Intuitively, we will know when we need to fix something in our child's world and when we simply need to listen. We can recognise the times when our child is whiny or their behaviour goes off-track, and we can slow down to make space for their feelings. We can set limits, allow them to laugh, cry or simply enjoy some special time to create the safety they need to show their feelings. With awareness of what's going on for them, we can help them get closer to their emotions rather than diverting them further away.

Recognising when we use distractions on ourselves

Healing ourselves is as much a part of this journey as listening to our children. It can help to bring some attention to the areas in our life where we might be distracting ourselves from our own feelings. We can think about what we do when we are feeling low, if we reach for some chocolate or coffee, or something stronger at the end of the day. We might try to keep busy, grab our phone, or surf the net.

I had always thought that having a cup of tea or coffee was a way to give me energy when I was tired. When I started listening time, however, I found that just talking about my exhaustion gave me energy, so I didn't feel the need for caffeine. I felt much more relaxed compared to when I took caffeine, as it made me feel nervous and edgy.

I realised that my exhaustion had been emotional as well as physical, and that my need for caffeine was an emotional one too. I had it when I was feeling a bit low, or when I was in a situation where I needed a confidence boost, such as going to a new parent-and-toddler group where I didn't know anyone.

I can remember the day after I had had a long listening session, I walked into the toddler group I had recently started going to feeling completely relaxed and at ease. I had released some of the feelings from old experiences that had chipped away at my confidence. I was no longer reliving them in the present. I could enjoy socialising without needing something to bolster me against the underlying feelings I had.

How connection heals addiction

A well-known scientific study found that if rats are given access to heroin or cocaine they will consume it until they die. From this it would seem obvious to conclude that heroin and cocaine are highly addictive and that rats, and, by extension, perhaps humans too, have no control once they become addicted. In a subsequent study, however, instead of the rats being kept in solitary cages, as they were previously, they lived together in a kind of rat heaven with wheels, coloured balls and delicious food. This time, when they were offered heroin, the rats didn't overdose and had much less interest in it.[2]

We can extrapolate this to humans: when life is hard and we lack pleasure and deep connection with other humans, and we are full of feelings, we try to cope in ways that are addictive, compulsive and that feel out of our control. When life is fun and bright, in contrast, and our environment is interesting and fulfilling, plus we have the important sense of connection with others, we don't need those addictions.

The feelings beneath our habits

This is not to say that anything is inherently bad or that we shouldn't enjoy ourselves. It's just that we should be aware of the habits we have that don't ultimately serve us very well; for example, perhaps we eat unhealthy food and then feel full and yucky. Or we spend too much time watching TV when deep down we know we'd feel better if we went for a walk or a swim.

Changing our habits need not be a struggle or about depriving ourselves of bad habits in a way that is painful or makes us unhappy. Our goal is to be happy and joyful, and to share that joy with our children. When we move through our feelings, rather than stopping them, we will find a much deeper happiness, just like our children do.

It takes time to undo the habit of stopping feelings and to begin allowing them instead. As children, we felt that there wasn't a place for us to take our feelings, so we tried to manage them. Now we need to consciously create a sense of safety and space in our lives so that we can feel.

We can take some time to be present to our emotions. Meditation, going for a quiet walk alone or having listening partnerships can all help. Perhaps we can schedule a listening time in the morning, or time to journal our thoughts and feelings in a notebook, and see how it feels to listen to ourselves, before having any caffeine or getting busy with the day. Gradually, we might find that we don't need so many pick-me-ups because our emotions are flowing more naturally.

I have found that when I am feeling good and have lots of listening time, I don't crave so many unhealthy foods or need caffeine so much. I have more energy and my mind is clearer, so I can think about healthy meals and snacks.

In listening partnerships, we can talk about the areas of our lives where we are struggling in the present. Releasing our feelings and tracing present struggles back to past hurts allows us to think more clearly about what to do in our current situation. We might see that it's possible to make changes to create the kind of life that we want. This in turn brings us a sense of joy and well-being so that we don't need to stop our feelings with addictions.

When uncomfortable feelings come up, we should notice them and remind ourselves that we don't need to make ourselves feel good immediately. Perhaps we can sit on the sofa for five minutes and notice the emotions until they pass. If they're more persistent, we could ask for some 'emergency' listening time. We can make an arrangement to try calling our listening partner when we notice we are feeling like comfort eating or drinking, or if we are trying to distract ourselves with our phone or the Internet.

It doesn't always come automatically to us to ask for help. We are used to dealing with feelings alone. But, if we can become aware of this tendency, we can consciously decide to change it and reach out to a listening partner.

There may be times when we are going through a lot of turmoil in our lives, and it's all we can do just to get through the day. As mentioned earlier in the book, when my daughter was two, my grandmother died, and I found that being a full-time mum gave me little time and space to process my grief. I was eating less healthily and drinking lots of caffeine, just to get through the day. I tried to get as much listening time as possible, but it still took a long time to release enough feelings so that I could change some of the habits I'd got into.

This is another reason why it's important to be kind to ourselves. We try to get by as best we can, and when we are ready we can try to be present to our feelings and reach out for support.

Have you noticed how when children are feeling good, they are completely in the present moment? They play, laugh and naturally just feel good and joyful. This is what we can return to when we move through our feelings. We will feel more energetic and clear-thinking when our minds aren't focusing on how to manage our pain. We'll be relaxed, rather than wired, and instead of being distracted by busyness, we'll be able to join our children feeling joy in the moment.

I have included the following case study, not because the parent does everything right in the situation but to show how things can become awkward and complicated when we try to stop children's feelings, and how listening often proves to be the best choice in the end.

Case Study: Jane

'My daughter had been to pre-school one day and then was going to a birthday party straight afterwards without me. When I picked her up from the party, she seemed quite disconnected. She wouldn't look me in the eye and just kept wanting to play. I got down on the floor and played Lego with her and some other girls, but I felt the play wasn't helping her to reconnect with me. I told her we needed to leave the party, and she said she would only go if she could take two balloons with her. Having used the Hand in Hand approach for a while I sensed that there was a tantrum brewing and that was the reason behind this request, but that day I really didn't feel like I had the capacity to listen to her in front of the whole party, nor did I want to disturb everyone, so I agreed to take the balloons.

'When we got to the car, she said, "Look I'm letting my balloons fly away." I was kind of distracted opening the car door, and when I turned around she had let them float away, and had started to cry. We got in the car, and she told me to start driving, I sensed that she wanted to distract herself now, but I said no, that we would wait a minute. I held her feet as she was kicking and getting really frustrated. She cried for a long time. Afterwards, we drove home and had a really lovely evening. We played and read books, and she was very connected and warm. She could look me in the eye again.'

EXERCISE: **Reflection – making connections with the past**

1 What do you do when you're feeling low? Do you reach for a coffee, chocolate or your phone? Write a list and talk about the history of these habits. When did they begin?

2 What are the biggest challenges you are facing in your life right now? Do these situations remind you of anything that happened earlier in your life?

3 What makes you feel good, and what made you feel good as a child? Take some time to do the things you love.

EXERCISE: Try this – think about what triggers feelings in your child

1 What are the safe, everyday situations that trigger feelings in your baby or toddler? Write a list and start to listen in these situations. Set a limit and listen to the feelings that come up in these situations.

2 In what kind of situations does your child get whiny or grumpy? How could they be opportunities for you to listen?

3 Notice times when your child asks for things and you sense it isn't about an immediate need but an underlying upset. Set a limit and listen.

4 Are there times when you need your child to do something, or you need to go somewhere and your child wants to play? Can you make some time to allow feelings and bring some laughter into the situation? Does it help your child to cooperate?

CHAPTER 6

Tear Histories and Cultures – The Story We Carry Within Us

•

'The deeper that sorrow carves into your being,
the more joy you can contain.'

Khalil Gibran, artist and poet

Throughout history, responses to crying have been extreme and negative. In the Middle Ages in Europe, crying or tantrumming was considered a sign that a child was possessed by the devil. Later, in the eighteenth century, crying was seen as evil and parents were advised to drive the wickedness out of children by breaking their will.[1]

These stories are examples from our history carried down to us from our ancestors. As each generation evolves, their attitudes and parenting practices become gentler and more child-centred. But the echoes of these historical views are still here in our present-day reactions. Crying is still seen as a negative behaviour that we should stop as quickly as possible, especially when we're out in public.

I hope, as you work through these chapters, that you're beginning to see your child's upsets in a different light. By now, you should be having lots of experiences of getting to the other side of your child's crying and seeing the healing benefits and closer connection between you and your child.

As you reach out to start your first listening partnership you'll also be having your own experience of releasing your feelings. All of that gives us the truth about crying. This knowledge, which has previously remained hidden, is that crying is a positive and natural way of expressing emotion.

These positive experiences help us to counteract the negative stories we've heard or experienced. But, at the end of the day, when our child has a meltdown because we served pasta instead of potatoes, all of this knowledge can go out the window.

Those negative stories can be pretty persistent. When our own stress response gets triggered we sometimes respond in ways that we aren't proud of, which seem to counteract everything we've learnt. We can go into a negative spiral, where we aren't able to respond with patience, and then we don't see the benefits in our family life.

Rethinking crying

There's a difference between thinking crying is OK, and actually feeling it. As well as changing our thoughts, we need to change how we feel and react in the moment.

We will have stressful situations, where we have multiple children crying or we're trying to juggle dinner and bedtime solo while listening to feelings, or our toddler's having a meltdown when we drop her off at day care and we need to get to work on time.

If we do get overwhelmed, our implicit memories about crying and upsets get reactivated. It can start to seem like there's something terribly wrong in the present when, in actual fact, it's our past memories talking. We might not know that's what is happening. All we know is that we want our child to stop crying as quickly as possible. We want to stop feeling so bad.

Our mind might make all kinds of rationalisations out of our stories. We might think that our children are wrong for crying or tantrumming, or that their reasons for getting upset are not valid. We might tell ourselves that they're just attention-seeking, or that they're acting spoilt, just trying to get what they want by making a fuss.

None of these rationalisations serves us, or our children, very well. They don't address their emotions or real reasons for crying. But they are there, due to the influence of our own history and the cultural reactions around us. When we are stressed, our pre-frontal cortex can't always function well, so we can't think clearly and act on what we've learnt about this healing process. Instead, we react emotionally based on past stories.

Our past remains with us

When we were children, we absorbed all the responses we received about crying: a kind of subtle, unconscious programming that, in most cases, it was a bad thing that must be stopped as quickly as possible.

We all have our individual stories about how our parents and other adults reacted to our upsets. As babies perhaps we were rocked or shushed, or given a dummy. As we got older and started to tantrum we might have been ignored, sent to our room, shouted at or hit.

We may have memories of being treated kindly when we cried, but even within these memories of kindness there is probably an element of trying to stop the upset. Even words said with love, such as 'Don't be sad', also carry another message: 'This outburst is too much for me and I can't handle it.' If a kind person with good intentions gave us a sweet or bought us a toy to cheer us up, it also comes with an underlying message, that we are meant to stop crying.

We may have verbal memories of what people said to us when we cried. There may also be subtle non-verbal responses at play. Because the limbic system is fully formed at birth, we pick up on our caregiver's subtle, non-verbal reactions to our tears, even before we can consciously interpret them.[2] If our mother got nervous or uncomfortable, we picked up on her tense body language. If someone continually gave us a dummy every time we got upset, we'd begin to internalise the idea that crying is not allowed.

Our stories about crying also get formed by observing how others were treated when they were upset and how this made us feel; for example, I remember coming home from holiday and my mother bursting into tears. I don't remember the full details of the memory, if my dad was there or how he was responding, but there was an atmosphere of despair. It seemed quite scary to me as a young child that my mum was crying.

Children get triggered by crying too, particularly if they haven't been listened to much. If they see other children or adults crying, their unexpressed emotions may get activated. If they haven't been listened to much themselves, they might tell another toddler to stop crying, or schoolchildren might call each other cry-babies if they get upset.

This is how a story is made, a tapestry of experiences that looks like an ultimate fact about crying. The view of crying as a negative behaviour that must be stopped is formed by our experiences.

How to deal with past stories in the present moment

When we think about our experiences as a child, we'll realise that our attitudes towards crying are not entirely our own. If our own history with crying was fraught, it's no wonder we react strongly when our children get upset. These stories we carry affect our actions, particularly when we are stressed.

If we can, it's important to remind ourselves that our negative reaction to crying is not about the present moment. We know that if we listen with warmth to our child until they finish crying, then afterwards they will be happier, more relaxed and cooperative. If we're finding it hard to listen, then it's probably our past stories talking.

When we experience negative thoughts and feelings about our child's upsets, we can try to bring ourselves back to the present moment. We can notice our reactions to their crying, if we can accept their bad mood, or if we find their behaviour or emotions challenging.

Taking a moment for ourselves can help us to work out what we need. We can take a few deep breaths, and remind ourselves about what we know about the healing power of tears. We should check in with ourselves and see if we have the patience to listen, or if we need to take some parental time out to calm down. We could sit on the sofa, or shut ourselves in the bathroom if our child is old enough to be left alone for a few minutes.

Allowing ourselves time to calm down helps to get our thinking brain – the pre-frontal cortex – working better again. Then we are there in the present, rather than wandering into past stories, and we can think more rationally about what to do.

Learning meditation or mindfulness can help. It gives us the skills to stay anchored in the present moment, staying calm and relaxed so that we don't get stressed and activate those implicit memories. Buddhist monk Thich Nhat Hanh recommends that meditators put a pebble in their pocket so that every time they notice it they remember to be mindful and in the present moment. We can try something similar for crying, using a pebble or visual reminder, so that in times of stress we remember to stay present and that tears are OK.

Allowing listening time to clarify our thoughts

These moments when we have to deal with our child's upsets or off-track behaviour are our healing opportunities. It might not seem that way at the time, but we can take the emotional debris that they trigger to our listening time.

With a listener we can talk about our childhood and how adults responded to us when we got upset, and how we tried to use our own natural healing process. As we talk, we'll release some of the tension related to these stories. We might find ourselves getting angry at how we were treated, and laugh or cry about the things we didn't heal from when we were younger because we didn't have anyone there to listen to us. We can create a new story where we have been heard and where our emotional responses have been accepted.

We won't remember all our experiences of crying, such as those from infancy, but these still affect us, and we can still heal from them. We still carry the implicit, emotional content of the memories, and we can try to access that in various ways.[3]

If other family members have told us something about how we were treated, we can talk about what they have said in a listening time. When my daughter was born, I found myself having conversations with my mum and dad about what it was like when I was young. My mum told me that when I was born I cried a lot for no reason. My dad attached a string to my crib so when I cried in the night he could rock it while in bed. When I was a toddler having a tantrum one day, my mum put me alone in the garden to try to calm me down.

Talking about the stories family members have told us about our infancy and childhood, with the warmth of a listener, can unlock strong feelings. We might laugh at some of the ways they reacted to us, perhaps thinking that we'd do something completely different. In that laughter is some of the tension and hurt that we've been carrying. We might also connect more deeply with the memory and cry as well.

We can be guided towards remembering our early feelings

Listening partners can ask questions, or give directions that help us access early feelings we can't consciously remember. Once in a listening time, when I was talking about my daughter's birth, my listening partner asked me what my own birth was like. The question seemed funny and ridiculous, and I laughed at first. But the warm and caring way my listening partner asked it triggered strong emotion in me. I then surprised myself by suddenly bursting into tears and coming out with, 'It wasn't what I expected.' Behind the words was a kind of grief, that the love and attention I had received didn't feel like enough. These feelings were a big surprise to me. Because our emotional brain is fully functional at birth, we do have implicit, unconscious memories of our early lives that can be recalled under certain circumstances, such as deep listening or under hypnosis. We may not recall the exact events, since the part of the brain that encodes conscious memory is not formed until the age of one, but we do carry the emotional content from our memories before this age. Many parents have found that when they are given the space to be deeply listened to they do have emotional reactions to things that happened before they can consciously remember.

Through many hours of listening to parents, and being listened to myself, it's clear that all of us come into the world expecting infinite love and attention and to be loved unconditionally. I realised it must have hurt to come into this world with a way of expressing feelings that my parents didn't understand. This is everybody's story, because a generation ago there was hardly any awareness of the healing power of tears in babies and children.

Although I didn't consciously remember the hurt, I had carried the feelings and could still access them and cry to heal. When we heal, the story doesn't change, but we no longer have to re-live it every time our children cry, or carry hurt feelings of rejection that lower our confidence and limit our lives.

Even if we don't have many memories to talk about, we can speculate about what might have happened based upon what we know about our parents and the other adults who took care of us. Just doing this can stir up emotions to talk about.

Our present reactions to our child's crying are like keys to release emotion, even when we have no conscious memories of why we react so strongly. We can talk about what's hard. Perhaps we struggle to set limits because we can't always handle the big upsets that come afterwards or we get really drained by our child's crying. These reactions give us clues to what our past experiences were like.

If we become frustrated by our child's crying, we can use listening time to vent our feelings. We can moan and complain, and release the locked-up emotion that is getting triggered by their upset.

Whether or not we cry easily often holds clues for how we were treated as infants and children, and the extent to which we were listened to. We can reflect on whether we find it easy to cry around other people or if we cry only with our spouse or a few trusted friends. We may cry more easily alone, because we got used to being sent away when we were acting off-track or expressing explosive emotions.

We might find it easier to cry in certain situations but not in others. This might be particularly true for men, who experience even more cultural pressure not to cry. Men may cry easily at a football match or watching a weepy in a darkened cinema, but feel uncomfortable crying in front of their family.

A safe place for our emotions

Not all of our present experiences provide the warmth and safety for us to express ourselves freely. We might sense that our loved ones aren't able to handle our emotions, so we hold them in. Listening partnerships are one relationship that is purposely designed for us to have the safety to share our feelings. If we find it hard to cry in front of a trusted listening partner, this is likely to be the influence of our past stories. Talking about what we can remember about crying, or how we may have been treated, can help as well as just making sure we have regular listening time each week.

As you release your backlog of emotions in listening time, it will become easier to separate your past stories about crying and upsets from your child's present emotional moments. Our attitude towards crying will slowly shift as we gather positive experiences of crying and being heard. It will become easier to cope with our child's upsets.

Our listening limits

After many experiences of my daughter crying and coming out the other side I now actually feel relief when she starts to cry. It's like after a hot day full of humidity when a big rainstorm clears the tension out of the air. If she's been whiny, impatient or clingy, I know these are all signs that she has feelings to release. When she has a big cry I know she'll be more peaceful afterwards.

It's not always easy though. Even when we do start listening to our child's upset, feeling patient and relaxed, we might find our patience draining if our child cries for a long time or has a lot of upsets.

There was a time when my daughter had a lot of meltdowns about tiny things. For days she would have meltdowns about the colour of her socks, always changing her mind about what colour she wanted. I would set limits, knowing that she needed to release some feelings, but there was only so much I could listen to. Sometimes I would rush out of the house, knowing the distraction of being outside would stop the feelings.

Life got a bit busier, and she stopped having big cries for a while, perhaps sensing that I wasn't resourced enough to handle it. I arranged for more listening time so that I felt better supported. When she started crying again, it was much easier to listen because I'd learnt and grown and been listened to myself.

Our past attitudes to crying produce a healthy response, in a sense. If we're getting angry and irritated by our child's crying, it makes sense to try to stop the crying as quickly as possible by bouncing or redirection, or whatever gentle methods work, so that we don't grow even more angry. We can then make an intention to obtain some listening time for ourselves to work on whatever feelings make crying hard for us to hear.

We'll always be playing catch-up. Our babies and toddlers are experts at this healing process while we're still relearning it. Telling our stories about crying helps us to listen to our children, and it also makes it easier for us to cry, so that we get to do our own healing too.

Case Study: Sally

'As an adult, I really didn't feel comfortable about crying with other people. During my listening time, I began talking about how hard it was to cry in front of others, how I wasn't sure about the listening process and if it was going to work for me. My listening partner asked me what it was like when I cried as a child.

'I remembered that when I was young, family members would often say to me that I looked really ugly when I cried. I started crying alone, or hiding my face whenever I was upset. I remember feeling really alone, that I couldn't show my upset to anyone.

'My listening partner gently encouraged me not to hide myself away as I talked, and that whatever feelings I had were welcome here. Over time I began to cry much more easily during my listening time.'

The following story demonstrates how talking about our own experience with crying helps to make it easier to listen to our children's feelings.

Case Study: Andrew

'I really hated it when my son cried. I felt compelled to stop him, and I didn't know why. I went to a workshop and tried out listening time, and the instructor asked me what it was like when I cried as a child. I told her that I didn't remember anything, but then suddenly this memory popped into my head.

'I remembered that my mother left me a lot with my grandmother, and that I often felt like crying when she went. I remembered that when I cried my grandmother would always take me out to look at the ducks and geese, and would always distract me by showing me things. I talked about how upset I felt that my grandmother wasn't listening, how isolated and alone I felt.

'I found it much easier to listen to my son after that.'

EXERCISE: **Reflection – remember when you cried as a child**

1 What happened when you cried in your family? Can you remember some specific instances? You can ask this

▶

question for other caregivers, such as a babysitter, nursery or school, if you can remember.

2 How do you feel when your child is crying? Angry, helpless or sad? How do you feel afterwards?

3 Think of some recent times when your child has had an upset. Let out all your feelings about it.

4 What is the response to crying in the culture that you come from? Think about your race/class/gender and how that has affected you.

5 Recall memories of crying, how did you feel? Did you try to stop yourself?

CHAPTER 7

The Journey Towards Sadness – Finding Our Tears Again

●

'Crying wasn't like riding a bike. Give it up, and
you quickly forget how it's done.'

Alice Hoffman, *The Ice Queen*

Ｗe were born with a natural healing process to recover
from our stress and upsets, but we weren't always able to
use it. As a result of having our tears stopped as children we don't
always cry easily as adults. We can, however, develop awareness
of our feelings, and by allowing them to flow more easily we can
recover our ability to cry. In this chapter I'll share more about
how we can find our tears again.

In my mid twenties I looked for ways to heal myself physically, through yoga, massage and meditation. I found that these
modalities also helped me emotionally. Through getting more
in touch with my body, I was able to allow my emotions to flow
so that I was no longer stuck and feeling angry but could access
the sadness underneath. At that point in time I didn't fully
understand the healing power of tears, but I did have the sense
that when I started crying I could finally let go of my emotions
and move on.

Like me, you may have been healing yourself through tears
without being consciously aware of it. You may have already

done things in your life that have helped you to get in touch with your body, access your emotions and, perhaps, cry. Dance, meditation, therapy or a heart-to-heart with a friend can all help to get our emotions flowing. Even if we don't cry in the moment, these activities contain the ingredients we need to begin healing. They allow us to slow down and be more aware of our bodies and our emotions, and if we are with other people, we also receive warm, human connection.

Allowing our natural healing process to take place

Our natural instinct to heal is still very much alive in our bodies and minds, even though there are sometimes opposing forces at work to repress our feelings. We might find that we already gravitate towards things that are good for our well-being and happen to contain one or more healing ingredients. Even something as simple as going for a walk alone in nature can be part of our healing path, because in the silence and peace we may become aware of what we are feeling. When my grandmother died I would often go for walks and start crying as soon as I was alone. In the quiet countryside there was space for my feelings.

I know that my body is a powerful key to how I am feeling, although I don't always listen to it. If I've spent too much time sitting at my desk writing this book, my body starts telling me with an aching neck and back. I sometimes continue writing, however, because my mind is telling me to get it finished. We sometimes do ignore what our body tells us, and by extension we are also ignoring its emotional signals.

We live in a world that doesn't allow much space for feelings. We have busy lives and are juggling many responsibilities. We may feel like we have to keep going, grab a coffee if we're really tired, and bottle up our feelings. When we are working or parenting over long hours, it might seem hard to listen to ourselves. We tend to ignore our own needs, and then the next thing we know is we've snapped or shouted and we're wondering where the anger or frustration came from.

It's understandable that we ignore our feelings. It's become a habit since our own feelings were often ignored when we were young. The first step to counteract this is to bring some attention to ourselves. In the same way that we slow down when we listen to our children's feelings, we can also slow down to become aware of our own.

Reconnecting with our feelings

Throughout the day, we can check in with ourselves and bring our awareness to our body. Perhaps we observe ourselves breathing for a few moments and notice the way our breath feels going in and out of our nostrils, and the rise and fall of our chest. This brings us back into our body, and closer to our feelings.

If the day seems long and we find ourselves repeatedly reaching for our phone, or reaching into our cupboards for our secret chocolate supply, we can then watch what feeling is behind that urge, and just notice it for a while. We don't always have a listening partner with us, but we do have this kind of inner listener who can be there, watching over us, as we are there with our children.

Anything that helps develop this inner listener to be more in the moment can help us heal. Yoga, meditation, listening partnerships, or just sitting quietly, can help you to be aware of your feelings – and it is the first step to getting them flowing.

The other big ingredient for getting our healing process started is a sense of warmth and connection with others. When children have regular attention in the form of special time or playlistening, it builds a sense of safety so that they feel connected enough to release their feelings. In order to cry freely, we need a sense of safety and connection too.

When we were upset as children and were acting off-track, our parents usually focused on what to do to control our behaviour, rather than on the feelings underneath. We may have been punished and isolated when we needed our parents the most.

We need to know that there are people who can really listen to us and connect to us on a deep level. It could be listening partners, friends or perhaps people we meet through our interests.

In my late twenties I joined a writing group, and a lot of the writers in it were sharing autobiographical work. I found myself shaking as I read my story aloud to the group, and strong, scary feelings rose to the surface. Although I didn't cry at that moment, the experience felt healing. I took away that sense of connection and that I had been heard and understood.

Each time we share big emotions with someone who is warm and completely present, it counteracts the times our upsets were not handled well and we were isolated.

How to encourage our tears

It can be extremely hard for us to reach out to others when we are upset. Because of our past history of being alone with our upsets, as well as societal attitudes, we can feel like we have to keep our misery to ourselves and not inflict it on others. If we are upset, it's good to remind ourselves of this tendency and to contact a trusted friend or listening partner if we can. These steps give us the warm, human connection we need for our feelings to flow.

Laughter and joy can be a wonderful pathway to finding tears, both inside and outside of listening partnerships. If we do find it hard to cry, we may actually need more joy in our lives and the laughter and human connection that comes along with it. We need to feel that all is well in the present to start releasing feelings about the times things weren't so good.

Some ways to ignite more laughter in our lives might include going to watch a comedy film or to see a live comedian, or arranging to meet up with friends whom we always enjoy laughing with. Sometimes it can seem like a struggle to arrange these things. Perhaps we're tired after a day of work or parenting, or our friends are busy with their families or lives. Talking in a listening partnership about what stands in the way of having a connected, joyful life can help. Clearing out some of the feelings can help us think more clearly about how to make a change in our lives, whether it's finding the courage to make a new friend or an energy boost to get us out in the evening.

We can also encourage our tears by seeking out things that make us cry. Perhaps we might rent a weepie film or listen to some sad music. Just curling up with this book might help your tears to flow, because the healing power will be in the forefront of your mind.

Unlocking your tears

There may have been times in the past when you tried to avoid your emotions, because you didn't want to cry. Once, while pregnant with my daughter, I was in the supermarket and there was an adorable six-month-old baby in the trolley in front of me. I found myself welling up with tears because it seemed so amazing that I would soon have a baby of my own. But I stopped myself from crying because it felt a bit embarrassing to be doing so in the supermarket queue! Perhaps, if I'd understood healing crying better, I would have given myself a moment to cry in a supermarket aisle, knowing that there was nothing wrong with being emotional.

After my daughter's birth I remember my husband playing music in the other room. I felt almost scared to listen to it – because I was in such an emotional state myself, I knew I would cry. Our emotions can seem scary when we're used to being alone with them, and so we can unconsciously avoid them.

Now we can try to treat moments like these differently, to notice if we get upset and allow ourselves to cry. We can stop what we are doing, so we aren't distracting ourselves, and just feel and make space for tears. If possible, it's good to find the support of another adult. If that's not possible, we can just sit with the feelings.

If our children are there, we can reassure them that we are just upset and will feel OK again in a moment. We don't need to hide our tears from them. As long as we're not crying too often around them, it's beneficial for them to witness us expressing our emotions in a healthy way.

When we need a listener

Often, we can't cry immediately. We are frustrated, angry or upset and there's something we need to talk about and work through to find our tears. The adults around us might be supportive of our feelings, or they might try to fix or offer solutions, or 'look on the bright side'. Their words might distract us from what we are feeling, so that we can't express ourselves freely.

We want to talk and communicate with our loved ones, but often our feelings end up getting tangled with theirs. They might get upset when we don't seem to want a solution or their help and may not understand that we just need to be listened to.

Our partners, friends or family might find it difficult to handle our feelings. If they haven't had their own experience of crying as a healing process, they might interpret the situation as something they need to fix or solve.

We can explain to our partners a little about what we have learnt about listening. Simply understanding the healing process can make them more accepting of our upset. Still, they might not be the best listeners, since the reality might be that they are actually more in need of a listener than we are.

When my daughter was a baby it often surprised me that I'd spend a day with her feeling fine and then as soon as my husband walked through the door, I'd suddenly feel exhausted, grumpy or start crying. It wasn't that I was that unhappy to see him! I realised that the feelings that were bottled up all day would spill out when he came through the door and that I was holding it all together until he got home.

I realised that if my feelings were regularly coming out in this way with my husband and in front of my daughter, it would be a good idea to get listening time at 5.30pm, just after he came home. It worked, and after a while of releasing my backlog of stress I didn't feel so overwhelmed by the end of each day. It was helpful advice to contain my feelings in a 'safe house' of listening time rather than letting them spill out in life.

As important as it is to share with the people who are central in our lives, it's also useful to get some in-depth help for our overwhelming emotions. It's like tidying away our emotions into a safe place instead of burying them or acting them out in life, which can get messy.

Listening partnerships are a wonderful way to reclaim our unshed tears. They are specifically designed to help us process our emotions, to laugh, cry and heal. The warmth and attention we receive acts as a powerful contradiction to the times when we were left alone with our upsets. It's often a higher level of warmth and attention than we ever get in everyday life because there is more time to focus on us and what we are feeling.

The benefit from exchanging feelings

It's helpful to share our feelings with someone in an exchange, because then we are both getting the listening we need to be good listeners. We sense our partner has attention to deal with our feelings, because they've dealt with their own. Then our tears can flow more easily.

Although crying alone can sometimes be beneficial, it's really the presence of another person that makes it safe for us to go more deeply into our feelings. Our partner can remain neutral and see a way out for us that we might not be aware of when we are caught up in sadness and despair.

It's often the words of our listening partner that will guide us out by counteracting our despair. They might encourage us when we struggle by reminding us, 'You can work this out.' Our partner can help us feel more hopeful, and sometimes that's just the trigger we need to start crying, as we let go of our feelings of hopelessness.

When we feel like the worst parent in the world, our listening partner might ask us about a time when we felt that we were doing a really good job or a time when we felt especially connected to our child. We might start crying when we realise that our feeling of being a bad parent is just a feeling that distorted our thinking and not the truth of how things really are. Our partner can help to show us that we are a good parent doing our best, and then we can find our tears.

The tears might take a while to flow

When you first start a listening partnership you might not start crying instantly. It takes time to undo the blocks and the ways in which we automatically try to stop our feelings. We might need some time to absorb our partner's warmth and attention, to gain the trust that they really do like us and are offering us unconditional support.

When I first started listening partnerships, I didn't cry that easily. Sometimes I found that talking stirred up my feelings, so I would cry a few hours later or the next day when I was alone, or perhaps with my husband. It took time to undo my self-consciousness and embarrassment about expressing feelings in 'public'. After nine months I gradually started crying with my listening partners. Now I cry much more easily and in front of my listening partners.

We can think of feelings as being like the layers of an onion that we gradually peel off, layer after layer, until we reach our deepest ones. At first we might just talk or laugh – or perhaps we will yawn, which releases physical tension. Whatever we do, it's all fine. As we continue to share our feelings we will be naturally led to our tears.

Tears are incredibly beneficial for us, but we'll still notice the benefits of listening partnerships, even if we're only talking about what's happening in our lives. There's no need to worry if we don't cry. This healing process should come naturally rather than being forced. If we have an urgency about crying, this creates tension rather than the relaxation we need for feelings to flow. You can simply be there in the present, noticing your thoughts, talking about whatever comes to mind. Over time, with the support of a listener, you will find your tears. Perhaps at first you'll be checking what you feel comfortable saying to your listening partner while you build safety and trust between the two of you. You might laugh a lot or just have a good moan. Again, that's all perfectly fine.

Moving towards sadness

To find sadness we often have to move through other emotions such as guilt, anger, fear and shame. We might find ourselves feeling uncomfortable and expressing more unattractive emotions, and we may wonder what our partner will think of us. In a good listening partnership, we'll gradually find that as time goes on and we build trust we will feel able to take more risks with what we disclose to each other. As our partner admits things that make them feel ashamed or embarrassed, we'll gradually feel safer to do the same.

Feeling the safety to express all our emotions honestly helps us to find the way to our sadness. If we struggle with this, we can remind ourselves that it's healthy to express these negative emotions in a safe space where they aren't targeted at anyone in particular, and, ironically, that expressing them is how we begin to let them go.

At the root of anger is almost always some sadness.[1] We couldn't express it at the time, and so we build a kind of tough armour to hide that vulnerability. Often, it's the full expression of that anger with a warm listener that allows us to access the sadness.

If something holds us back from sharing our emotions, we can ask ourselves what it is. Perhaps it's embarrassment or shame at feeling certain things. Perhaps we feel anger at our own parents and feel guilty about expressing it when we know that if we compare our childhood to someone else's we recognise that it could have been much worse. Or we sometimes feel anger towards our child but we don't want to admit it.

We can feel free to reveal any emotions

It's good to remember that whatever we feel is OK. Our emotions are all totally valid and acceptable. We didn't choose these emotions, but there is a reason and a story behind them that we need to tell. We can be proud of ourselves to be expressing them in a safe space, so that they don't interfere with our lives and we can be our best possible self for our family.

There may be some especially hard subjects that we avoid during our listening time: perhaps something that doesn't seem to have a solution so we have buried and ignored it. It could be trauma from the past or difficulties in the present; for example, we feel grief that there's no possibility of our child going to the pre-school we love, or that we can't afford to have another child. Because these subjects seem to have no solution, it feels useless to talk about them.

It can be particularly helpful to dive into these painful subjects, as our tears often lie at the heart of them. If we truly allow ourselves to feel the grief, we may find that we have a shift in perspective that makes us feel less pain about the situation, or it's possible that if we do clear our head of the emotion a little we will be able to see a solution.

The connection we need to cry

If you're finding that you're doing lots of listening partnerships, but you aren't crying, then it could be that you need some more warmth and connection with your listening partner in order to let the feelings go. You may be subconsciously avoiding connection, for example, by not making eye contact or by looking away when you get to a subject that is hard to talk about.

We get into the habit of avoiding connection because we were often disconnected from others in the past when we had strong feelings. Our feelings might make us unconsciously move away from connection; for example, if we feel embarrassed or ashamed about what we are talking about.

If we find it hard to find our feelings, and find ourselves getting lost in thinking with our mind rather than being present with our partner, we can bring ourselves back to the moment, perhaps look them in the eye, and then notice how we feel. Getting in-person listening time can help, because the sense of a person really being there is much stronger. But if that's not possible, regular phone or Skype sessions are still much better than trying to do Hand in Hand Parenting without any listening for ourselves at all.

Sometimes it's helpful not to think about what to talk about, but instead to notice what your body feels, and then see what pops into your head when you are connected to your physical self. Thoughts that come to us suddenly are often ones that spring up from our deep feelings, and may seem forbidden, risky or embarrassing. We can try to talk about these things – or even just thinking about telling the forbidden might be enough to get us laughing with embarrassment and get the healing process going.

It's so essential that we go through this process of recovering our own tears. Through them we become better listeners for our children. We can also grow and find joy through being parents, rather than becoming stuck with negative emotions. Each time we cry we can get all of our negative feelings out of the way and return again and again to the love we have for our children.

Case Study: Amy

'I started a listening partnership with my friend who had already been doing them for a while. I felt really jealous that she could cry, as I just couldn't seem to. For the first six months I would work on my everyday difficulties, and then something shifted in me. I began to go deeper into the process. My listening partner asked me questions about how my present difficulties related to my past. I also began to automatically search for a past memory that related to my present difficulty. It was when I started delving fully into my past that I began to cry much more easily.'

EXERCISE: Reflection – feeling your emotions

1 Shut your eyes and notice your breath, notice how your body feels sitting in a chair, count the breaths. Can you get in touch with the emotion you are feeling in this moment? Try this process with a listening partner and talk about what you notice.

2 When negative emotions are interfering with your day, try sitting quietly for a few moments. Notice how the emotion passes after a while.

3 During listening time, if you feel a strong emotion, ask yourself where you feel the feeling in your body, make a sound to express the feeling, such as a moan or a scream. You can ask your partner to do the same when they have a strong feeling too.

4 In which situations do you feel comfortable to cry? In which situations do you not feel comfortable?

EXERCISE: Try this – free writing

'We are all writers, just as we are all talkers', according to Pat Schneider, a creative-writing teacher who believes everyone has their own distinct writing voice.

1   Choose a time that suits you when you can find space when nobody else is around: perhaps first thing in the morning or last thing at night when the rest of your family are sleeping.

2   Write your thoughts down in a journal. Describe what you can see, hear and smell. Notice your breathing, and write whatever thoughts pop into your head. Follow your train of thought. Notice all those little thoughts that you might normally push away.

3   Continue for 10–15 minutes, or however long you want to.

Regular practice in listening to yourself helps you to get in touch with your intuition and instincts, and to hear that little voice inside your head that knows deep down what to do in any given situation – and also knows how to heal.

EXERCISE: Try this – tips for recovering your tears

1   Watch your favourite weepie film. Ask friends to recommend some too.

2   Are there any songs that make you cry? Take some time to be alone and listen to them. Ask friends what their favourite sad song is.

3   Read an emotional poem. Ask any book-loving friends you know for recommendations.

▶

4 Look at old photographs from the past. Perhaps talk with some old friends or family about them, or show them to a listening partner.

CHAPTER 8

The Baby Stage – First Steps in Listening

•

'Making the decision to have a child is
momentous. It is to decide forever to have your
heart go walking around outside your body.'

Elizabeth Stone

Our babies are born, and our parenting journey begins.
In those first few weeks and months as a new parent we
might feel a whole range of feelings from joy and love to confusion, exhaustion, or of being overwhelmed.

If you're reading this book and haven't given birth yet, it's
a great time to set up a listening partnership. You can take the
time to get to know someone before life gets hectic. It can also
be really helpful to share and release some of the excitement
and anxiety that you feel about the birth and becoming a
parent.

Starting a listening partnership may not be an easy thing to
do in those first few months after your baby's birth. One alternative is to keep a notebook by your bed and jot down thoughts
and feelings whenever you get the chance. If you find yourself
getting emotional, it's good to allow yourself space for the feelings to flow. Having a partner or family member to talk and cry
with whenever you need to can be very supportive.

Our baby's crying seems like an obvious way to measure our success as new parents. We feel like we're doing a good job when we can work out what our baby wants. We can often feel inadequate if we can't stop them from crying.

Our culture often encourages us to define our babies and children by the extent to which they express their emotions. 'Good' babies are quiet and happy, smiling all the time. 'Difficult' babies express themselves loudly and are harder to please.

We can be a little kinder to ourselves and our families. We know our babies are born fundamentally good and that if they're whiny or upset, they have a need, or they simply need to cry. We also know that we're good parents doing our best too. The fact that you are taking the time to read this book shows that you care deeply about your child's emotional well-being and happiness.

When your baby is born, especially if you are a first-time parent, you'll be using a lot of trial and error as you work through your list of needs, trying to work out what your baby wants. In those blurry days and months of first-time parenthood, you might not have much time for reading this book, having a regular listening partnership or following the advice given here to the letter. In those first few months, you will be getting to know your baby and yourself as a parent, and you're using one of the most important parenting tools you have: your own instincts.

There are some parenting methods out there that advocate strict feeding or sleeping schedules that go against parenting instincts and our need to nurture our babies. There is a wealth of parenting information out there that can leave us feeling confused or trying things that go against our own instincts.

When my daughter was born I read about attachment parenting. It's an approach where we have a close physical connection with our babies most of the time. Some of the attachment-parenting books I read implied that I should be carrying my baby in a sling the whole time, but then another book said that babies need lots of freedom of movement to explore their world. In the end, with such contradictory advice being recommended by experts, I could only take what information made sense to me, and then make my own judgement about what felt right to me to follow for my daughter at any given moment.

The need to cry

When your baby cries, you'll go through your checklist of needs to work out what they want. As it's not always easy to work out what they need, it's always good to err on the side of caution; for example, try to feed your baby even if you're not sure whether he is hungry or to check his nappy even if you've recently changed it. Your baby can't use words. He can't tell you that his tummy hurts or that he's too cold.

Within this checklist of needs we should also include the need to cry. It can sometimes feel like instinct to stop our babies from crying, even though they don't seem to have a particular need that we can identify. Within our instincts to love and nurture our baby, we also have the unconscious influence of our past stories: how our parents or caregivers reacted to our crying. These stories can influence our response to crying, so that we often try to stop it without being aware of what we are doing.

When my daughter was a newborn, I'd sometimes have moments when I was trying to feed her but she kept coming off the breast, or I'd be pacing around the house because that was the only way to get her to stop crying. I would then suddenly realise that my attempts to stop her from crying weren't meeting an actual need that she had, and that it was possible she simply needed to cry.

As we have seen, the limbic system – the home of emotions – is fully developed before birth, and therefore our babies feel and experience a lot and have an emotional life that is as rich and complex as our own. All babies will experience some kind of stress or upset. It could be a stressful pregnancy, a difficult birth or medical intervention, or just the minor, everyday stress of living in a stimulating, fast-paced world.

Birth's imprint

Healing is important, because the way we come into the world leaves a powerful imprint on us. Thomas Verny is a psychiatrist who researched how birth is a profound experience that shapes our character. In his book *The Secret Life of the Unborn Child* he concluded that 'if we are happier, or sadder, angrier, or more depressed than other people, it is at least in part, as a result of the way we were born'.

Through working with his patients he found that although they didn't remember their birth consciously, they could recall what happened under hypnosis. This suggests that they did carry the unconscious memories of their pre-natal and birth life. They carried the emotional content with them and this affected their lives.[1]

I don't think anything about our child's destiny is as fixed as Verny's research suggests. When *The Secret Life of the Unborn Child* was published in the 1980s, it was not widely understood that crying is healing. Bonding and connecting with our babies is the foundation for processing and overcoming challenging experiences.

The correlation between the level of stress of mothers in pregnancy to how much crying infants did suggests that a baby will need to cry more if he or she has had stressful experiences.[2] Even if the pregnancy and birth was completely uneventful, the baby will still inevitably experience some stress and upset as a natural part of life.

While writing this book, my aunt told me that when my cousin was a baby she had cried for three-hour stretches at a time. During those crying spells she couldn't seem to do anything to cheer her up. Over time she remembered how she had been in transition in labour for three hours. In between cries she knew that her baby was happy and at ease, so my aunt intuitively sensed that the crying was helping her baby. She accepted these crying spells and just waited for them to pass.

Three hours is a long time to listen, and not all babies cry so much, but it's actually normal for babies to have a big cry each day, often in the evening. If we try to stop the feelings, they become stored up and carried into toddlerhood. If we can listen now, we help our baby to heal without carrying the feelings for any longer than is necessary.

Learning to decipher our baby's crying

When I look back at my daughter's infancy, I realise there were times when I was simplifying her emotions and assuming that she was crying because she was tired or hungry when in actual fact she was crying to express her emotions.

One time I was at a baby group and my daughter was complaining. I assumed she was tired, and so we left. Afterwards she was perfectly happy and content and didn't fall asleep for ages. It was only then that I realised that being in the group made her feel uncomfortable and that perhaps she found it too stimulating, or she was picking up on my own feelings of not being completely comfortable in a group of mothers I didn't know well. Even though our babies can't have complex conversations with us about how they feel, they are actually just as emotional as us.

When we get stressed as new parents, we tend to react based on our emotions and past stories about crying. It's at these times that we might find ourselves trying to stop our baby from crying, even when their only need is to express how they are feeling.

Beginning to listen

When your baby cries, it helps if you can bring your awareness into the present moment. You can notice if you are meeting a particular need or if you are simply trying to stop your baby from crying for the sake of it. If she doesn't have a need but won't stop crying, you can just hold her, look at her and reassure her. Whenever possible, it helps to sit still and just be there with your baby's upset, so that she gets the sense that you accept her crying.

Crying can evoke strong emotional reactions in us. We wonder if we've met all our baby's needs and if we're doing it in the right way. It can be that everything is fine in the present and that our baby is healing from past hurts. Crying can also be a sign that something is really wrong in the present, however. If you have any doubts or worries, you should always contact a doctor or health visitor.

Crying, even of the positive, healing kind can be hard for us to listen to. We may wonder what has hurt our baby so much, and as we run our minds through the possibilities we might feel guilty or responsible. When my daughter cried a lot in the evenings, I would think of her birth and feel enormous regret that it hadn't been the natural, drug-free birth I had hoped for.

Even though I'd acted in her best interests at the time, I was still saddened by the thought that things could have been different. Getting listening time, even months afterwards, helped me to release the regret and guilt that I felt. Then my mind was freed up to listen to her.

Listening time also helps when our own past stories make it hard to listen to crying. We can talk about the emotions our baby's crying triggers in us, and what it feels like to become a parent. We can let out some of our stress and frustration, nerves or worries, or whatever it is that makes it hard. Then we can be calmer in the moment.

As mentioned in the last chapter, we can use listening time to talk about what our own birth was like or how our parents treated us as babies and reacted to our crying, if we know anything about it.

If we can find a good moment to ask our parents, or anyone who knew us as babies, then this can be helpful, but it's not essential. Just speculating on what it might have been like for us as newborns can sometimes bring up laughter and tears. This can help to heal some of the feelings that get triggered now we have become a parent ourselves.

When we have talked about the past, and have laughed and cried a little ourselves, then our instincts are freed of these stories. It then becomes a lot easier to work out when we just need to listen to our baby.

How we inadvertently stop babies from expressing their feelings

After getting to know our babies, and focusing on the important stuff such as learning to be a parent and keeping our baby alive, we might find that we've got into a habit of stopping the crying without even being consciously aware of it. These patterns are common, even inevitable. We are just beginning to learn how to listen to feelings and we weren't listened to ourselves.

My pattern was feeding my daughter to sleep. When she was younger and frequently hungry, I fed her a lot, and it just became a habit after those first few months. When she was two months old, she went through a stage where she wouldn't feed to sleep, so either my husband or I would pace around the house holding her until, after a while, she was sleepy enough to feed to sleep.

Occasionally it struck me that I could just sit and hold her and allow her to cry. But if she cried a lot I would think that something was wrong and wonder if she was hungry, then feed her again. This became a pattern and I would automatically feed her to sleep every night.

Babies naturally release feelings before and after sleep, which I talk more about in Chapter 13.[3] Because our culture has instilled in us the idea that when babies cry there is always something wrong in the present, we confuse our baby's crying because they are upset with being tired and needing to sleep. In fact, they often let go of feelings before sleep so that they can naturally sleep more easily.

I remember that part of the reason I fell into a pattern of stopping my daughter from crying was because there were times when I doubted what I read: were tears really healing? Why was no one else talking about it? Sifting through my thoughts, and working out what was right, was such an important part of the process because I could then parent in a way that felt right to me, rather than simply following something that was written down in a book. (And this also applies to this one!)

By the time I started my Hand in Hand instructor training I was ready to work out how to listen to my daughter's feelings. I had a regular listening partnership in place, and support and information to help me work out much more clearly when I was stopping her from crying.

Listening time can help us to notice the ways in which we respond to our babies and if we've got caught in any patterns. Some common ways may be feeding to sleep, rocking, bouncing or giving an older baby a dummy just to keep him quiet. During listening time we can follow our train of thought, telling our past stories and releasing our feelings, trusting our judgement that we can work out what to do.

One night, it might then make sense to us not to rock or feed our baby to sleep (only if they are not hungry of course). We can tell him that we are not going to feed him or rock him, and then listen instead. He might cry for a long time when we begin to listen, because he has a backlog of feelings from the times we didn't know how to listen. It's OK that we didn't listen from the beginning, and our baby can catch up on his crying. We can notice when he is in a better mood afterwards or if he sleeps for longer.

Consistency is overrated

There might be times when you cannot listen to your baby's crying, when you run out of patience or time. Sometimes the best thing to do for yourself is to take your baby out in a sling to fall asleep or give her a dummy.

Consistency is actually a much overrated aspect of how we create emotional safety for our children. Having a rhythm or routine to our days is fine, and it can help our babies and toddlers feel safe and secure. But, in actual fact, when babies and toddlers have their feelings listened to, their security comes from a much deeper place, from knowing that whatever happens there will always be an adult to take care of their emotional needs. When babies and toddlers are listened to, they are much more able to adapt to life's changes.[4]

Perhaps one day we might feed our baby to sleep, perhaps another day we listen to the feelings. We do what feels right and best at that moment. Every time we listen, it helps our baby to release feelings. The main thing is that our baby has what they most need when they cry: our warm presence to let them know that they are safe.

Knowing that crying was healing was such a gift to me when my daughter was young. It really helped my confidence as a new mum to know that sometimes when she cried the most important thing I could do was just to hold her in my arms and listen. It was a relief to know that she had this way to let her feelings go. Sometimes I shed a few tears with her; we were healing together.

Case Study: Kelly

'When my son was eight months old he was really clingy and wouldn't be held by anyone. One day I wanted to spend the afternoon with my older kids, because I felt they were really suffering from a lack of attention since he'd been born. I told my baby that he would spend time with grandma. He started crying and then buried his face in my chest, then he abruptly stopped.

'I gently manoeuvred him away from me so that I could look into his eyes. He started crying again. I reassured him that he would be fine and safe with grandma. He cried for a while, and then was fine playing with his grandma when I told him I was leaving with his siblings to go to the park. He was really happy to see me when I returned again.'

EXERCISE: Reflection – think about your baby's birth and crying, and your own childhood

1   How does your baby's crying make you feel?

2   Do you know how your parents reacted to your crying when you were a child? You could ask them if you think they wouldn't mind talking about it.

3   Tell the story of your child's birth. Even if you have told it before, talk about it again and again, as much as you need to let go of the feelings you have about it.

CHAPTER 9

The Broken-cookie Phenomenon – How Our Children's Emotions Work

•

'One's suffering disappears when one lets oneself
go, when one yields – even to sadness.'

Antoine de Saint-Exupéry,
author of *The Little Prince*

Have you ever noticed how small things can trigger enormous upset in your baby or toddler? With a young baby it could be something as simple as putting a hat on them or pulling clothes over their head. All those little everyday moments can trigger crying and upsets. Our babies have only just come into the world, and the sensations, sights and smells are completely new. It's no wonder they get easily overwhelmed and cry about things that would be no big deal to an adult.

With a toddler, the reasons they cry can seem silly and petty, and we may have less patience and empathy for them when they're no longer babies. Perhaps they wanted a blue cup instead of a red cup. Or they want you to spoon some porridge into their bowl, and then change their mind and start crying, saying they wanted to do it themselves. It can feel like you can't win trying to meet the demands of an extremely fussy toddler.

Our toddlers aren't actually as petty or over-emotional as it might appear. Aletha Solter coined the term 'broken-cookie phenomenon' to describe how babies and children often use small reasons as a pretext to release bigger feelings about deeper hurts.

Adults are no different really. When my grandmother died, I travelled to London to go to her funeral. When I got there I realised I had forgotten the dress that I was going to wear. I burst into tears. The other adults around me immediately tried to think up solutions: a last-minute shopping trip the next day or an outfit borrowed from my sister.

I stopped crying, since I didn't want to make everyone else feel uncomfortable. I knew that I didn't really want a solution and that the crying wasn't really about the dress but about my grief that my grandmother had died. My natural healing process was at work.

It was late, so I went into the bedroom where I was sleeping. My husband stayed with me as I started crying again. Luckily, he understood and was able to listen to me. I cried for a long time, perhaps 30 minutes or longer. It was only when I took off what I was wearing to go to bed that I realised that the dress I had on would be fine to wear to the funeral. While I had been in the midst of the upset, I hadn't even thought about it.

The next day I was able to read a poem at the funeral, and I felt strong and composed. In a sense, forgetting the dress was a blessing, as it gave me the chance to let go of at least some of the grief.

How small things can hide other worries

Our common cultural perception of toddlers is that they are often completely inflexible, stubborn over small things and miniature dictators. Children are naturally assertive when they feel safe to be so, and they will have strong opinions. No amount of listening to feelings could ever dampen our child's naturally strong-willed spirit. It might be challenging for us as parents, but it will serve them well in adulthood.

I think that it's important that we fulfil our child's requests and needs as much as we can. Being able to have their preferences heard and have a say in what goes on in their lives helps to build their confidence and independence. Each time they choose their cup or bowl they're learning to choose for themselves and make decisions. It's inevitable, however, that there will be times when things don't end up exactly the way our child wants; for example, we need to use the lift and forget that she always loves to press the button, or we buy the wrong kind of juice.

When babies and toddlers are free of feelings, they can cooperate with us, and can actually deal with small disappointments, change and transitions. This can seem hard to believe. Because the healing power of tears isn't widely known, a lot of toddlers don't get the chance to let their feelings out very often. Many toddlers are on the brink of an upset most of the time.

When children are free of feelings, their pre-frontal cortex works well so that they can think clearly. They can listen to our explanation that it's probably a good idea to go out wearing their wellington boots because it has been raining a lot recently, and they will probably want to jump in puddles.

When a child is upset, their pre-frontal cortex isn't working as well, so they might have a meltdown about wearing wellington boots because they already had some upset feelings. They can't listen to our rationalising and our explanation of why wearing boots is a good idea.

My daughter's favourite colour is blue. She'll often request a blue cup and, most of the time, I'll give it to her. Sometimes we are in a rush and I can't find the blue cup. Most of the time, she'll saying something like, 'That's OK Mummy. I'll have a pink one.' Her flexibility surprises me because we don't expect our toddlers to be this way. But they can be when their feelings are regularly listened to. Occasionally, she will cry about it, and I realise it was probably a good thing I couldn't find the blue cup, because it gave her a chance to let out some feelings.

I'm amazed when my daughter doesn't cry during moments we would typically associate with big meltdowns; for example, when her balloon floated away or when we lost a toy dog on the train. When she does get upset, I help her to fully let out her feelings, which means she doesn't need to use every slightly upsetting situation to release big feelings.

The traditional parenting view of broken cookies

Traditional parenting has two different ways of dealing with broken-cookie situations. In one scenario we give in about the small stuff because we want to avoid tantrums. We let a child 'have their way'. After all, it's not that hard just to go into the cupboard and find the right colour spoon or cup. We might sigh with frustration and feel resentful at having to give in to their every whim, but we want our child to be happy, and it's hard to deal with the emotional fallout when they're not.

When we avoid these broken-cookie situations, by trying to please our children, we're not actually making them happy but only postponing their sadness. We're also making our parent- ing job harder, because our child might continue to try to have upsets over small things. We might find ourselves constantly trying to use avoidance tactics to prevent a meltdown. In the meantime, our child will act out their feelings in aggression, whining or other off-track behaviour.

In the second scenario we say no to the request, because we don't want to give in again. Our child has a meltdown, but we find it really hard to muster empathy or cuddles because they are crying about something that is so small. We also might feel that we don't want to encourage their crying about such a tiny thing. We might use distraction or redirection to cheer them up, or ignore the crying and just get on with whatever we're doing.

It's likely that if our child did get upset about something small, then there is a bigger reason. If they can't continue to cry for as long as they need to with our warmth and empathy, the bigger upset doesn't get healed. So this approach also makes parenting much harder than it needs to be.

The third way: listening

The most effective long-term approach is to listen. It allows broken-cookie moments to be turned into positive healing experiences. In the long run your child will be less grumpy and whiny and have many fewer mini-meltdowns because they are able to get their feelings out fully each time.

When our baby or toddler gets upset we can assess the situation. Is something really wrong in the present, or is it just feelings bubbling up that are attached to a broken cookie? If they've been grumpy and irritable before having the meltdown, the apparent need for the blue cup might just be a trigger for deeper feelings.

We can slow down and stay in that moment. We can notice if we are feeling a sense of rush and panic, and are unconsciously trying to avoid an upset.

If our toddler gets upset because we didn't give them the blue cup, then we can look at them and give them a hug, and gently say something like, 'I know you really wanted that cup. I think you'll be fine with the red cup.' Emphasising and listening, rather than frantically searching around for the blue cup, is a much more connected way of being with our child. We can help them with the feelings that made them so attached to having that particular cup.

Setting limits with broken cookies

There may be times when your child isn't crying but is grumpy and irritable and seems quite rigid in their requests; for example, they want their knife and fork exactly straight, or they won't eat the porridge because we made it with small oats instead of big ones, or they want to wear a particular dress even though it's dirty. You might notice that if you try to fix these situations, and make it exactly how your child wants it, then she will remain grumpy. It can seem that she is looking for something to get upset about, and in fact this is exactly what she is doing, at least on an unconscious level.

During these moments, it's more beneficial to look at what your child needs rather than her surface 'want'. You can set a limit and say no. You can say, 'I'm sure you'll be fine with your knife like this,' or 'I'm sorry, but these are the only oats we've got today.' Then she can let out whatever feelings are making it seem like the world will fall apart if things aren't exactly the way she wants them. Afterwards, she will probably become more flexible and see the current situation differently. When the bigger feelings are gone she might feel brave enough to try porridge with a different kind of oat, or find another outfit she likes.

Focus on just one moment

If there are days when your child is in a bad mood, then choosing one broken-cookie moment to listen can completely turn the day around. A bad mood can simply be over in a moment when we allow our children to let go of their feelings instead of leaving them stuck.

Even young babies have their own broken-cookie moments. All sorts of everyday situations can trigger crying, which might relate to bigger fears or upsets.

A common scenario might be that your baby picks up an object that is unsafe and you take it away from him. Babies do have a natural desire to explore, discover and learn, and they need freedom in childproof environments to do so; however, there are times when we will need to set a limit to keep them safe. When babies are relaxed and happy, they can also listen to our explanations of why we need to take an object away, and they might be happy to cooperate even though they don't fully understand our words.

If we need to take an object away from them, we might automatically do so quickly and then try to distract them with something else in an attempt to avoid their upset. This can result in a baby building up frustration. It could even shorten their attention span, making it more likely that they'll get distracted and bored, because they are used to having their explorations interrupted abruptly and controlled by an adult.

If we need to take something away, we should do it slowly and gradually. We should look at our baby and tell them what we are doing. This gives them the space to express whatever upset they feel. They might have a build-up of feelings, such as frustration and powerlessness, from other times when they were exploring and we needed to set a limit.

We can give them something else to play with when they've finished crying, or just let them explore and discover something themselves afterwards. Listening to babies in each moment means that they don't build up stress and frustration. It helps to reduce toddler tantrums or behavioural issues as they grow older.

The bigger reason behind the broken cookie

Children may never say what the real reason for their crying is, and although that might be frustrating for us, we can still listen. Sometimes we might have a clue about what the bigger reason could be, which can make it easier to spot a broken-cookie moment.

When my daughter was three, she started going to a playgroup and she suddenly seemed to want to be independent. She moved into her own room by her own choice, and she started carrying her own little rucksack with her everywhere, just like she did at the playgroup. She became determined to put on her own clothes and shoes, and she refused my help.

I let her do many things for herself, knowing that this helped her to build confidence. But I also began to see that doing things for herself was becoming a broken cookie. Sometimes, I noticed there were a lot of strong feelings in these moments. If I picked up her shoe she would grab it from me desperately. It occurred to me that although she enjoyed the playgroup she might also have some feelings of hurt as she got used to the fact that I wasn't always around to help her. I imagined that when she was there she would have to wait for help with her clothes and shoes. The teachers would be helping nine other children as well, which would be a very new experience for her that might trigger feelings of being alone.

One evening, I had her pyjamas in my hand and was just about to help her put them on when she grabbed them from me. I decided to hold on to them.

'I can help you with them,' I said. She immediately started to cry.

'I want to do it myself', she said.

'I just want you to know that I will always be there to help you, if you need me.' She started crying, saying, 'No, no.' I listened to her, and then when the crying died down I explained, 'And if I'm not there, like when you're at playgroup, then your teachers can help you.' She had another wave of crying.

'There will always be someone there to help you. And most of the time, I'll be there to help you.'

And then she said, 'Even when I'm 18?'

'Yes,' I said.

'Even when I'm 19?'

I said, 'Yes.'

After each question she would cry and cry with relief. It suddenly occurred to me what else had been bothering her. When we were travelling by public transport we had been talking about the older school children and teenagers who didn't always have their parents with them. We had talked about when she was older she could go to places by herself and wouldn't always need me around.

The thought of growing up and becoming independent, along with the separation at her playgroup, had caused some anxiety about the future. Because I'd sensed what was bothering her, I could set a limit. It opened up the space for her to cry, and for us to talk about her worries. I could reassure her that we could still stay close, even when she got older. It was such a beautiful conversation, and a way to rebuild our closeness after the separation.

After that her desperate need to do absolutely everything for herself had gone. She was very huggy with me. We felt closer together, even though she was away from me a couple of mornings a week. I knew she'd be more confident about exploring her independence, now that she felt reassured that we would still be just as close, even as she set off into the world.

Listening time can help us to keep calm

Broken-cookie moments can really push our buttons. When your child is crying because he doesn't want to wear red socks, it's not always easy to remember that there is probably a bigger reason for his upset. Listening time can help. You can vent some uncensored frustration. It can be helpful to ask yourself, or a listening partner could ask you, what would have happened if you had a big cry about something small when you were a child?

Remember that we can only help our children with their feelings when we feel calm and patient ourselves. If our batteries are running low, or we are in a rush and can't listen, then we can 'please' our children and fix the situation. We can get them an unbroken cookie, or the colour cup they want. We can make a mental note to get some listening time for ourselves, or spend some one-to-one time with our child so that they get another chance to tell us how they are feeling.

Whenever possible, it's good to listen. Sparing a few minutes can reduce off-track behaviour and make a difference to our child's mood and the rest of the day. In the long run, listening to all those broken-cookie moments gives our children the healing they need, so that they don't try over and over again to pick upsets about every little thing, and when they're free of upsets we can discover just how flexible a toddler can be.

Multiple meltdowns

If your child is going through a stage of having a lot of broken-cookie moments, it's especially important for you to have listening time. As well as giving you the attention you need to be a calm, patient listener, it also helps you to reflect on what's going on in you and your child's life.

It could be that if you've just started listening to her feelings, your child might sense your availability and will start clearing out a backlog of emotions. If this is the case, over time there will be fewer upsets.

Having a lot of meltdowns about small things can sometimes simply be a sign that your child is finding the pace of life overwhelming; for example, if she's adjusting to a new day-care situation, she might need more downtime than normal.

It's good also to check what's going on in their lives: if they are happy at nursery or if they are processing any big changes like moving house or the birth of a sibling. Asking a toddler directly isn't easy, and asking a baby is obviously impossible! But if they're getting frequently upset and don't seem to be feeling better, it could be that we might need to look at aspects in their life, such as diet, health or the quality of any childcare, which could all be important factors that can affect a child's moods.

Through special time and playlistening we can listen to our children's stories about what is going on. During our own listening time we can process our own thoughts and feelings to help us work out what to do in any given situation; for example, if your child is wanting to pretend to be a baby all the time, and a new sibling has just been born, listening time could help you reflect on this so that you can be mindful about your child's feelings or come up with creative solutions so that she feels important and valued too.

Adult broken cookies

As I explained with my story about the dress, the broken-cookie phenomenon doesn't just apply to children. Perhaps it's living in a culture that doesn't allow much space for feelings that means we tend to hold them in until a particular trigger causes us to explode.

If you're at home all day trying to be patient and calm with your child, or at work trying to be polite to your colleagues, by the end of the day you might have gathered a certain level of stress and tension. When your partner walks through the door, something they do or say might trigger anger or we might sense that we now have an available listener and an upset comes flooding out.

Regular listening time helps to lighten the load of our own feelings so that we don't so often get to breaking point. If you find that you're having frequent upsets or angry outbursts, it's a good idea to organise more listening time so that instead of being surprised by your emotions at random moments you have a safe space where you can take them so that they don't interfere with your life.

You'll then find that when you need to have that important conversation with your spouse about a parenting issue, or with your boss about having more flexible working hours, you'll be more likely to be calm and rational, and be able to communicate effectively.

It's also important to remember the principle of broken cookies in your listening time. If you are complaining about a hurt because a friend has let you down, or you had an argument with your partner, it might be that a past issue that hasn't been healed is what makes the present harder to deal with. If you heal this earlier hurt, it will become easier to work out what to do in the present. We can remember to ask ourselves if this situation reminds us of anything from our past. If our listening partner is the one struggling, we can ask them this question too.

We don't need to deny our broken-cookie moments as something petty and small. We can acknowledge them in the same way that we do for our children. As children, we might have been told to grow up or stop being so immature, so we internalise this lack of empathy for our own emotional states. We think that because we are adults we shouldn't get upset about something small; for example, if we are jealous of a friend who we think is more popular than we are, we might push these feelings away, thinking that they are childish. It's good to acknowledge all our feelings, no matter how petty and small we judge them to be. It's good to remember there may be a bigger hurt that makes the current situation hard, even if we can't consciously remember it. It's actually embracing all of our emotions that makes us feel heard so that we can let them go. A good listening partner can unconditionally accept our emotions and help us to do the same. Then we'll have renewed patience for our children's broken-cookie moments.

Case Study: Louise

'When my daughter was three we spent a lovely long summer day playing in the park with lots of friends. At the end of the day she told me she wanted an ice cream. We bought one and the ice cream vendor handed it to her.

'She then said, no, she wanted me to hand it to her. I sensed then that perhaps a meltdown was brewing, because it seemed like a kind of fussy request, and normally she'd have just eaten the ice cream happily. She then decided she didn't want it; she wanted another kind of ice cream. I told her we're not going to get another kind. She started crying; I held her, and said I was sorry, giving her lots of warmth and empathy, even though I wasn't going to get her another ice cream.

'She fell asleep in her buggy on the way home, and the next day she was in a great mood again. Before I learnt about Hand in Hand Parenting I would have tried to make her happy in whatever way possible, even if that meant constantly trying to dodge her whining and moaning, and the threat of a meltdown. It was so much more relaxing to be able to just listen and help this natural process restore her good mood again.'

EXERCISE: Reflection – setting limits

1 What are some common scenarios in which you need to set limits with your child?

2 How do you feel when you need to set limits?

3 Have you had any of your own broken-cookie moments recently? What were they?

EXERCISE: Try this: watching for broken-cookie moments

Look out for broken-cookie moments with your child and set limits if you sense they have a deeper, underlying upset.

CHAPTER 10

Special Time – Creating the Safety for Tears

•

'The present moment is filled with joy and
happiness. If you are attentive, you will see it.'

Thich Nhat Hanh, Buddhist monk

Children cry to heal when they feel connected to us, when
they feel safe and trust that we are there to listen. But
they don't always cry freely when they have upsets. Often it's
their off-track behaviour that alerts us to the fact that they are
having trouble with their emotions. Once we have learnt how to
set limits and how to notice when our children need to release
their feelings, there may still be times when we sense they have
feelings under the surface that we can't seem to help them with.

It's inevitable that our children won't always release their feelings freely. We live in a culture that doesn't fully acknowledge
children's need to express themselves, and we are still learning to
listen to them ourselves. Even though our babies were born with
the innate ability to use this natural healing process, we might
not have known how to fully listen from the very beginning. In
our busy lives, there will inevitably be times when we can't fully
be there for our children on a deep emotional level.

Children seem to have an intuitive sense of when we are
available. I remember hosting a group listening time with two

friends. After we returned to our families, each one of us had a child who ended up having a big cry about something. Our children's limbic system sensed that our cups were full and that we could listen well. When we get in the mindset of thinking that we need to fix our child's off-track behaviour, the first step actually might be to fix ourselves with a big dose of listening time.

Utilising special time

Special time is another way in which we can give our child the message that we're available to listen. Often, just giving children a dose of connection makes it a little safer to let go of their feelings.

Special time is one-to-one time that you spend with your child, following their lead and doing whatever they choose. To begin special time, first decide how much time you have available to give your child. It's important to think not just about the literal amount of time you have, but also how much time you feel emotionally able to give.

Special time can be fun for both parent and child, but it can also be draining for us to give such concentrated one-to-one attention. We might not have spent much one-to-one time with our own parents. They probably had cooking or cleaning to do or work outside the home. If they did spend time with us, they probably didn't follow everything we wanted to do and probably tried to direct the play in some way. There may well have also been other siblings around.

We can only give to the extent we've experienced being given to ourselves. Listening time helps us refuel, so that we receive the warm uninterrupted attention that we want to give.

How to give special time

To begin, you tell your child that it's special time and that they have x number of minutes to do whatever they want with you. You follow their lead, showering them with attention, giving them lots of eye contact and affection.

During special time, we don't multitask. We don't tidy up their toy cupboard or check the dinner while they're playing Lego. We should turn our mobile phone off and make sure we aren't interrupted.

Special time is different from the regular quality time we spend with our children, such as reading bedtime stories or cuddling up in the morning, although these times are very important too.

During special time, the child gets to choose what to do herself and fully directs the play. This is time when we can slow right down and go at our child's pace. It's great to choose a time when you have energy and are free of responsibilities so that you can simply enjoy the company of your child. If you have several children who are still young, choose a time when there is another adult around to look after the others, so that it really is just one-to-one time.

During the play we should normally only set limits for safety reasons. We should follow our child's lead completely. If, for example, she wants to play a board game or do a puzzle, we don't give suggestions about how to do it correctly, or if she wants to read a book, we don't give suggestions about which one to choose.

This is an important power reversal, which is a welcome relief to the times when kids have to spend time doing what we need to do and complying with our schedules. Children get to be completely self-directed with our warm attention and presence. It's no wonder my daughter says special time is her favourite thing to do!

When children experience themselves as powerful, it acts as a powerful contradiction to the times when they were hurt. In most situations, where there is stress or trauma there is also a feeling of being powerless to stop it. This reversal allows children to build their confidence.

Special time for babies

You can introduce special time at any age, even before your baby really understands the concept. You can tell your baby that you're going to do special time, and set a timer. Even with a newborn, you can do special time where you hold your baby on your lap or lying next to you, and gaze into each other's eyes or play a game of peek-a-boo. When it's done regularly, your baby will learn to recognise the words and understand that this is their time to have your full attention.

I started doing special time with my daughter when she was about nine months old. By 11 months old she would crawl off and explore as soon as I said the words 'special time', knowing that I'd follow her. She would often choose to crawl out of our apartment, exploring the lift or the hallway. Knowing what special time was, and knowing she'd have my full attention, gave her the confidence to be more adventurous than she would normally be. We will see with older children as well that they feel safe to take risks and explore new things within the safety of our warm attention.

Using a timer

Some parents have told me that they find the idea of using a timer slightly artificial, but it's a very important part of the process. The timer gives both you and your child a clear idea of how long special time is. When we first start doing special time, it can seem quite intimidating to have a long stretch of time in front of us where we lose ourselves in our child's play. The timer helps it to feel more manageable.

At first I found giving special time hard. I started in short bursts and gradually, as I nurtured myself with regular listening partnerships, I was able to give more time.

I find that the timer creates a magical time for my daughter and myself. I'm not getting distracted by thoughts of when should I stop playing to make dinner or tidy up. The timer governs time instead of me, so I'm able to fully focus on her.

Perhaps this is why special time actually feels like a meditation. As thoughts of my to-do list flash through my mind, I let them go and return to my daughter. I've noticed that if I'm feeling a little bit low, ten minutes of special time with my daughter can actually brighten my mood.

That's the secret of special time. It's not just for the benefit of our children. We need that sense of close connection with them too, and it's where the joy of parenting lies.

As parents, we want nothing more than to see our children happy, and special time gives them what they need most: to be free to do what they love with our warm attention. Because of the way the mirror neurons work, we absorb their joy, and feel it too. (I talked about mirror neurons in Chapter 2, page 32.)

Special time for off-track behaviour

Special time is ideal for when our child is clingy or displaying any kind of off-track behaviour. It's not our first reaction, because when we were off-track as children, we might have been punished, ignored or shouted at. We might need a lot of listening time to keep our pre-frontal cortex in thinking mode during these moments, so that we can remember that what our child really needs is our warm attention. When my daughter is behaving in ways that irritate me, I try to remind myself that she probably needs connection, and I try to do a spontaneous special time as and when I can. This often works as an instant soothing balm, because she immediately gets what she's asking for with her off-track behaviour: connection with me.

The stories our children show us during special time

Sometimes children will show us something that they are going through in special time. When my daughter started playgroup, she loved to pretend to be a baby during special time, lying in my arms and making baby noises. I tried to do this as much as I could, to nurture that part of her that needed more time being close to me before venturing off into the world.

During special time, we might discover that there are opportunities for playlistening with our child so that we can help them to heal from the issues they bring to us in the play. When my daughter was working on feelings about separation, she liked to play a game where her hands were the baby hands and my hands were the mummy hands.

At first I found the game quite annoying, having her hands clinging to mine all the time. Then one day I found a way to bring laughter into the game. When the 'baby hands' went away from the 'mummy hands' I would say, 'I hope they don't run too far away', with a playful tone in my voice, inviting her to make the hands run away. When they did, I would playfully exclaim, 'Oh! That's too far', and chase them. I would grab them gently, and pull them back to wherever we had been sitting, playfully turning the situation around so that I was the clingy one who needed her babies close. This would elicit a lot of laughter.

Sometimes, special time is like a warm-up for playlistening. As we enter into our child's world of play we can notice the themes they bring up. We may intuitively sense how to help them to release feelings through laughter.

Crying after special time

After special time your child might start to cry. He might feel disappointed that special time is over, or perhaps something happens immediately after special time that turns into a broken-cookie moment. This can be disheartening for us. We've spent the time and effort being with our child and doing something that they love, and now they are crying because they didn't get enough special time or because we have to go and cook dinner. It can appear as if our children are spoilt and ungrateful or impossibly needy; however, usually the opposite is true.

During special time our child gets to experience himself as powerful, and his confidence and sense of being loved builds as we shower him with warm attention. This counteracts the times when he got hurt, where he didn't feel fully connected to us or in control. After absorbing our attention, upset feelings might bubble up to the surface. Our child senses that we are there to listen to him and help him heal. When special time ends, those feelings might spill out.

Once, my daughter and I did a lovely, long special time where she pretended to be a baby. Shortly afterwards she started crying, because she wanted me to pick her up, but I couldn't because I had bags of shopping in my hands.

I sensed that she was not physically tired but that her need to be picked up came from the feelings she had been working through. Perhaps she was pretending to be a baby because she still had some feelings of hurt remaining from when she was small and helpless. These feelings were being triggered by her growing independence, as if something was holding her back.

I decided to set a limit. I knelt down, looked in her eyes, and told her that I couldn't pick her up. She cried for a few minutes, and I hugged her. She was then happy to walk, running off down the underpass at the train station, which she loves to do. I could help her with the feelings that were getting in the way of her fully embracing growing older and enjoying her independence.

A spoiled outing?

Crying after special time can be what is known as the 'spoiled-outing phenomenon'.[1] A common parenting scenario might be that you take your child on an outing and do lots of things that she loves, with lots of close connections with family. Towards the end of the day, she'll have a big meltdown about something. It can appear that she has been totally ungrateful for everything you've done, and has now decided to ruin the day.

If we look at this scenario from a healing perspective, however, it's very different. Your child has absorbed all of your closeness and connection. She might feel that she wants the fun to continue even though she's partly tired and worn out from the day. She has had some wonderful experiences that might trigger memories from past times that weren't so wonderful. Her limbic system may sense that this is a good time to let some of these old hurts go because she feels your presence and attention.

When we understand this healing process we can see these tears in a more positive light. Your child is trying to let go of negative emotions that get in the way of her enjoying life and cooperating with the other adults and children around her. When we listen with empathy we'll have a more cooperative child afterwards.

It's good to make sure that we save some time and some of our own emotional energy in case our child has an upset after special time finishes. They may not cry immediately after the special time, but there may be an upset later in the day or the next day. It's good to be aware that it might happen.

Like much of what I explain in this book, it applies to our own emotions as well. When we see our own emotions in a different light we can empathise and understand our child's emotions better too.

Learning about the spoiled-outing phenomenon has given me an awareness of times when my own feelings bubble up, and I feel like something is wrong, but that it could be just that I'm healing from past hurt.

One time I hosted a party and had fun with a wonderful, connected group of people. Later, I started crying after everyone had left. I suddenly felt incredibly lonely. It didn't make sense, until I realised that the party had contradicted feelings of loneliness that I'd carried from times when I hadn't felt so well connected to people. This contradiction gave me an opportunity to heal.

Regular special time

When we start doing special time we should think about how we can make it a regular occurrence in our family life. How many children do we have? What sort of other commitments do we have and how much time do we have available?

The first thing to realise is that even if you have a busy life there is still room for special time. I read an inspiring story of a woman with seven children, and each child had a day of the week for special time. I read another interesting story of how a working mum gave her daughter five minutes of special time each morning before she went to work. Because special time is such a concentrated form of attention, even a small amount can make a difference.

The other point to realise is that special time, like all of the other listening tools, is an investment that pays off. It's all part of how we help our children's feelings to flow naturally so that they have a greater sense of well-being. That way, when we need them to get dressed in a hurry, they are more likely to cooperate because they feel well connected and their feelings aren't getting in the way. Using the Hand in Hand Parenting tools proactively will actually save us time in the long run.

It's a bit like tidying up the house. If you don't do it very often, and don't put things back where they belong, the mess builds up. The time we spend sifting through things, trying to remember where we put them, ends up taking more time than the actual tidying up would.

If we don't spend time investing in our child's emotional needs with special time, playlistening and staylistening, when we need to get something done in a hurry and need our child's cooperation, we'll have to wade through the emotional mess to get it. It takes more time than if we invest the time in using the tools to start with.

Having said that, special time should not be another reason for us to feel guilty. If we're not doing special time, or we're doing it half-heartedly and not enjoying it, the first step is to nurture ourselves. We can be really kind to ourselves and ask ourselves what *we* need so that we will have the energy to give special time wholeheartedly. Listening time can help to clear the mind so that we can work out how to get special time into our routine.

Special time can trigger a lot of feelings in us, because we didn't get this kind of play while we were young. Perhaps our child chooses a kind of play that we don't like and we find it really boring. Listening time can help us release the feelings that get in the way of just delighting in what our child is doing, whether it's playing endless Lego or role-playing at shops. Try using your listening time to moan about how much you dislike your child's choice of what to play in special time. You might find that next time, when your feelings are out of the way, it will be much easier to enjoy something just because your child enjoys it.

I've often finished my listening time and given my daughter special time immediately afterwards. When I feel more connected and supported with my feelings it is much easier to be present with my daughter.

The life of our dreams

Special time can be hard for us if we aren't getting enough time in our life to do what we love to do. We can use listening time as thinking time to work out what's in the way of us doing what we love, and if there's a way we can change this. Or it can be time to work out what we'd like to do for ourselves. Perhaps we really love painting pictures or want to train to be a yoga instructor. In this way, being there for our child pushes us to heal whatever stands in the way of living the life of our dreams.

Exchanging special time with our listening partner can also help. I tried this at a Hand in Hand Parenting retreat. Everyone was inside exchanging special time, and I decided my partner and I would go out for a walk in the country air. It felt amazing to have some time to do what I really wanted to do with a companion who'd go along with whatever I chose.

I had often felt guilty for not giving my daughter enough special time or enough playlistening, always feeling my own internal pressure to give more and more. But experiencing special time just once made me realise what a big gift it is just to give our child our full attention in this way.

If days go by without giving special time, then you can still create the close connection you need with your child for healing to take place. You can still have the bedtime stories, or cuddles in the morning, as well as spontaneous moments of playfulness and laughter. Then, after some listening time for yourself, you can start to introduce special time again.

A simple way to connect to other issues

Special time might seem like small stuff, but it paves the way to connecting about the big stuff. When we get down on the floor with our child, it gives them the sense that we are there for them, and they feel safety and trust to tell us about the big stuff.

One evening I did special time before my daughter's bedtime; this was unusual because we normally do it in the morning. I helped her put all of her dolls and teddies to bed, then when we got into bed, she asked me, 'How did I get in your tummy with all the food in there?' What followed was a lot of questions about pregnancy and birth. I described step by step what happened during the birth in an age-appropriate way. I wanted to be honest, but I also didn't want to flood her system with any information that would be overwhelming. The birth had been long and difficult and at one point her heart rate had dropped very low. I left that part out. I gave a short sentence or two of information for every question she asked so that she felt in control of the conversation.

At one point, she looked upset, and I asked her, 'Did it feel scary to you? I'm really sorry it was scary.' She burst into tears and I hugged her. I explained that it wasn't meant to feel scary, it was meant to feel safe. She cried for a while, and then asked some more questions.

I explained how when she was born they put her on my chest. She cried when I told her this, and then asked what happened next. I explained that the doctors needed to check her, so her dad had carried her to the other side of the room. She cried, and I told her that her dad had been with her the whole time, that he'd been holding her hand and talking to her. This made her cry even more. I explained how after that they gave her back to me and she slept in the bed with me the whole night. She cried with relief. 'What happened next,' she asked. I explained how the next day she had woken up and smiled at me. She cried about that too.

My daughter was a Peppa Pig fan, and a few days later she watched all the way through an episode where one of the characters goes to hospital, and later one about the doctor. Until we'd had that healing conversation, she had been too afraid to watch them. It began simply with special time.

As our children get older we can continue to do special time into the teenage years. We can spend time just being, making the space that says, I'm available if you want to talk, or laugh or cry, I'm here.

Case Study: Lynn

'I did special time with my daughter just after eating lunch. We had a really nice time playing and laughing together. When the special time finished, she immediately asked for some milk and bread. I have noticed that she often uses food as a way to deal with her emotions, and it seemed obvious to me that she was using food to cope with her sadness that the special time was over.

'I told her no, that we couldn't have any milk or bread because she'd just had lunch. She started crying. She said that I never played with her, and that the special time had been horrible and that we never did nice stuff together. I didn't take her outburst too personally, as we had just had a lovely special time together and it seemed like it was just the hurt feelings talking.

'I listened until she finished crying, then she was in a great mood, happily playing with me and her sister. She didn't get hungry for ages after that.'

EXERCISE: Reflection – thinking more about one-to-one time

1 Talk or write about how special time is going. Describe the feelings that come up for you.

2 Can you remember spending one-to-one time with your parents when you were young? How did it feel?

EXERCISE: Try this – experimenting with special time

1   Give special time to your child. Start with 10–15 minutes.
    Notice how much time you feel genuinely able to give, and
    experiment with different lengths. Can you make it a regular
    part of your schedule?

2   Try special time with a listening partner in person. Receiving
    listening yourself makes it much easier to give.

CHAPTER 11

What's Laughter Got to Do With It? Emotional Release, the Fun Way

•

'Laughter is the shortest distance
between two people.'

Victor Borge

Why devote a whole chapter to laughter in a book about tears? Laughter is like the fun sister of tears. Laughter plays a role in emotional release, as we have touched upon in previous chapters. We let go of light fears and embarrassment with giggles. Sometimes, in a situation where our child's not cooperating, all we need to do is to get them laughing in order to dissolve the power struggle.

The Hand in Hand Parenting tool of playlistening is where we pick up on what makes our child laugh while they are in the more powerful role. We have probably all naturally done some form of playlistening with our children; for example, in a game of peek-a-boo, when we pretend to be surprised to see our baby again, or hide-and-seek where we pretend we can't find our toddler while they giggle behind a curtain.

The main difference with playlistening is that we are more conscious of what we are doing, and we try to do more of it. We repeat whatever makes our child laugh to really get the giggles flowing. We follow their lead, so that they are always powerful and in control. As mentioned earlier, no tickling is allowed. Although tickling elicits laughter, it is involuntary and a result of our child being uncomfortable and powerless in the present.

Playlistening is anything where we are silly, make mistakes or give our child the power. We try to get dressed and put our trousers on our head instead of our legs. We allow our child to push us off the bed or sofa, and fall onto the floor looking shocked at their immense strength. We try to brush their teeth and end up brushing our own nose or ears instead. We act with naive surprise when we realise that we've been doing it wrongly.

Babies and toddlers can feel very powerless at times. They see adults as all-powerful and competent while they are still learning to do the things we can do with ease. In the situations where they were hurt, or when they get stressed and tense, there was most likely an element of powerlessness.

Playlistening reverses this because the child is always in control. These situations are a powerful antidote to times when they have felt helpless. It's a welcome relief if we put on our jumper inside out with the label showing, or put the milk away in the cupboard instead of the fridge, and exclaim at our mistakes.

Sometimes, playlistening might start off as a genuine mistake we made while distracted or preoccupied. We can repeat the mistake again and again, or perhaps vary the theme; for example, with the milk we might say, 'Oh, I shouldn't put the milk away in the cupboard, I'll put it away in the bathroom', and then realise our mistake and try a different location, again and again as their laughter flows.

Playlistening can be great to sprinkle laughter here and there throughout our day. Or we can do a longer playlistening session if we continue to find things that will make our child laugh. If we have more time, we can create wild variations on whatever makes them laugh in order to elicit more and more laughter.

My daughter and I played a game where she would push me

off the bed. At first I would just fall on the floor, and this would be enough to make her laugh. After we'd been playing for a while I decided to fly off the bed, as if my daughter was so strong that she had kicked me into the bathroom, the living room or even out of the front door. My daughter would run after me laughing and laughing in delight at how far I flew.

Whether we create a giggle-fest for our child or just a few laughs, it's all part of encouraging their natural healing process. Laughter helps them release the feelings that can get in the way of feeling close to us, and wanting to cooperate with us. Experiencing themselves as powerful helps them to build their confidence in the real world.

Beginning playlistening

It's very simple to begin playlistening. Just notice what makes your child laugh, and repeat whatever you're doing. There are some games that seem to almost universally get the giggles flowing, and I've included a list at the end of the chapter that you can try out.

Laughter is also individual to each child. The things that make a child laugh can relate to the kind of fears and anxieties they have or the things they are learning.

When children are learning to walk, they can find it really funny if we try to walk and fall over. Or if they are getting frustrated trying to learn how to put clothes on they might find it funny if we try to put our clothes on and get all in a tangle, or put our socks on our hands, or trousers on our arms. Laughing about the things they find hard can help to build their resilience so that they keep trying.

A while back I planned a long trip to catch up with friends and family in the UK. When I told my daughter about it, and all the places we were going, she told me that we were going to too many places and seeing too many people.

Although she enjoys the adventure of travel, the change in routine can bring up strong feelings. It's tiring to meet a lot of people she doesn't remember, or has never met before.

I suddenly had the idea to make a joke out of it. I invented nonsense places, and told her we were going to sipsy and ooglewood, and we were going to meet people like igglepop and bifflebosh. Soon she was laughing and laughing, and releasing some of the tension and anxiety about travelling. She coped well with the actual trip, and relished meeting everyone and all the attention she got.

Laughter can help with a child's fears

Once, we were on a train playing with my phone. My daughter would make up a name, like it's Nona calling, or it's Loola. I would answer the phone, and exclaim, 'I don't know you', and then hang up, pretending to be scared about talking to someone I didn't know. She laughed a lot. I imagine she was releasing some of the tension she feels around people she doesn't know.

Laughter allows us to hold our child's hand, and go a little closer to what scares them. Laugh by laugh they become a little less scared.

Laughter can also help release the tension surrounding other kinds of issues. When my daughter was going through a phase where she had trouble sharing, we played a game in the park, where I would throw a ball and then her dad and I would chase after it. We would all exclaim 'Mine! Mine! Mine!' then, just at the last minute, we would always let her get the ball. This really made her laugh, particularly if her dad or I put up a big struggle and tried, but failed, to get the ball. Working through the issue in play made her much more relaxed about sharing in real-life situations.

We don't actually have to be consciously aware of the issue our child is working on when they're laughing. Just picking up on whatever makes them laugh while they're in the more powerful role can be healing.

Rough-and-tumble

Playing at rough-and-tumble (or roughhousing) is another good way to get the giggles flowing. Studies have found that regular rough-and-tumble helps brain development and reduces aggression.[1]

It's important to follow our child's lead, and play in a way that isn't physically overpowering. We can chase our child in a playful way but always let them escape. Or we catch them and give them kisses. We can give our toddler a horsey-back ride on the bed and then drop them into a pile of cushions. We can notice when our toddler laughs and says 'Again!' or tells us what they want to do. We can stop if they tell us to stop, or notice the signs that our child doesn't like the play.

We may not have experienced this kind of play when we were young. The grown-ups in our childhood may have played in ways that might have been fun but sometimes felt overwhelming to us. They might have tickled us when we didn't like it, overpowered us or turned into a scary monster. We may have enjoyed aspects of this play, partly because children crave this kind of attention and connection from adults. But this kind of play doesn't provide children with the healing experience of feeling powerful themselves. This kind of play might come automatically to us, until we reflect on our past experiences.

It's good to be mindful and check whether the physical play we're engaging in allows our child to be powerful and that we're not physically overpowering them.

Occasionally, I still find myself playing in ways that are more about exerting power than giving power to my daughter; for example, when my daughter was three she went through an obsession with my breasts and was always trying to grab them. For a while she seemed to use this play as a kind of security blanket. One day I grabbed her and turned her upside down in an attempt to be playful. She laughed at first, but then she started screaming and told me to stop. I stopped immediately and noticed that it was my frustration with her behaviour that was making me play in that way. I was trying to exert my power to get her to stop. I realised that I needed to think of a more creative way to diffuse the situation, in a way that made her feel powerful and connected rather than physically overwhelmed.

Listening time – how did adults play with us in the past?

We can arrange for listening time where we talk about the way adults played with us, and this can free our minds up to play physically in a way that makes our child feel powerful and competent. We also need to have some time to feel physically competent ourselves. Dancing, yoga or other activities can help us feel more playful. Fun wrestling with a listening partner or friend we know well might seem like a silly idea but it can be a really good way of getting in touch with our playful nature. Or you could try to have a competition to see who can pull off the other person's socks first!

When we play physically with our kids, but let them have the power and remain in control, it counteracts the times when they felt physically threatened or out of control.

Aggression in play

Our children might bring up aggression in their play, which is probably a response to times when they felt scared. When my daughter was one year old and went through a biting stage, I found myself playing a game with her where she would make her hand into a claw shape, and move to scratch my face while I was holding her. I would catch her hand, smile and playfully say, 'Oh, you're my lovely sweet baby, so sweet and gentle.' We did it again and again, and she would laugh each time. Shortly after that the biting stage came to an end.

If our child brings aggression into the play, it helps if we can respond in a playful way while setting limits, catching a hand or foot that's about to scratch or kick with a warm smile or a playful tone. This gives our child a big dose of unconditional love, so that they know that we accept even their most difficult feelings. Playing like this means that it's less likely the aggression will come out in real situations with other children. We can set limits that let our child know that real, hard hitting or kicking is unacceptable, such as saying in a warm tone, 'No, no, no, I can't let you hit me.' Play like this helps to release the fear behind the aggression. If we find ourselves getting angry or irritated and not being able to respond in a playful way, it's usually a good idea to stop the play. Later, we can get some listening time about whatever feelings came up for us.

Laugh away off-track behaviour

When our child is feeling disconnected or acting in an off-track way, laughter can help release the tension behind their behaviour and rebuild closeness. If our child is refusing to do something like brush their teeth or get dressed, a few moments of laughter can completely turn the situation around. At other times, his behaviour might be more challenging, but every little bit of laughter is like a stepping stone towards cooperation. I'm always amazed how laughter can diffuse tension and turn a situation around. Knowing this, laughter is the best discipline tool we have.

When my daughter was two years old, she went shopping with her dad every Saturday, which she loved. One morning, she refused to get dressed even though she had been excited about going. I found myself explaining in a logical manner that if she wanted to go she needed to get dressed or she would miss the train, but she just didn't seem to process what I was telling her.

I realised that the fundamental mistake I was making was trying to communicate with her in words. Her pre-frontal cortex wasn't functioning well because her limbic system was full of feelings. I needed to speak in the language of emotion instead.

I put her socks on her hands, or on my feet, or her skirt on her head. Each time I would exclaim, 'Oh no, that's not right!' She would laugh and laugh. I started to dress her teddy, and then took him to the front door saying, 'Come on, it's time to go.' Then when I got to the door I would exclaim, 'Oh! That's not my girl, that's teddy.' She found this hilarious. I repeated it, and she laughed and laughed. After playing for a while she happily got dressed.

It seems counterintuitive that when we want to rush to get something done we should slow down to laugh and connect, but on most occasions it's actually quicker because it addresses the feelings that are making it hard for our child to cooperate.

When my daughter was three I needed her to take some hay-fever medicine. I knew she would find it a bit strange, as it was one that you spray into your mouth. I tried it myself, and found that it tasted like oregano. I didn't want to lie to her, as she is very sensitive to taste, so I told her it tasted a bit herby and a bit strong.

Then I had an idea. I tried to take it myself, but instead I sprayed it on funny places, like my armpits, or my nose or ears. Every time I did it I looked really surprised at my mistake. She laughed and laughed. Soon her mouth was wide open ready to try the medicine. She tried it, and thought the taste was a bit yucky, but after five minutes she was exclaiming she felt better.

Prevent off-track behaviour through laughter

If we can be playful around our child's off-track behaviour and get them laughing, then they'll get their need met for connection and release some of the tension behind their actions. They will then be less likely to behave in that way in the future.

My daughter went through a stage of pulling the magnetic

letters off the fridge and throwing them onto the floor. At first I felt a flash of irritation, but then I tried to remind myself that she must not be feeling good to behave in that way. I thought it through, and realised that I could easily let this behaviour go since it wasn't too disruptive. Nothing important was going to get damaged. I could play around it without getting too triggered, so I exclaimed in a playful way, so that she knew I wasn't really annoyed, 'Hey! Who threw these magnetic letters on the floor? I must put them back.'

I put them all back, and then walked away saying to myself, 'I hope nobody does that again.' Then I walked away and acted all surprised when she pulled them onto the floor again.

Common parenting wisdom suggests that if we give children attention for being 'naughty', we just encourage more of that behaviour. Well, this is true, but only in the short term. My daughter did pull off the letters again and again, laughing as I pretended to be annoyed and enjoying the attention. In the long term though, it makes that behaviour less likely because she's released a lot of the feelings that were behind it. After she laughed and soaked up my warm attention, the game had served its purpose and she moved on to doing something else.

Children can understand the difference between a game and when it's serious. Our children know us. They have a strong sense of right and wrong just from learning and observing and living with us. They know we like to keep a tidy house and that we don't like objects broken or damaged.

If they're feeling off-track they might pull books off the shelves, knowing that it will push our buttons and get our attention. If we allow them to do so, and turn it into a game that gets laughter flowing (or redirect it to something we're not worried about damaging, like Duplo), then it doesn't mean they're going to behave like this all the time. The opposite is true in fact: if children get lots of time to be their natural playful selves, they'll feel more connected to us and will be less likely to seek our attention in off-track ways.

Like the other Hand in Hand Parenting listening tools, any time we do playlistening with our children it's an investment of time. Playlistening melts away all the feelings of frustration and irritation. Afterwards, our child will probably happily cooperate and also be more likely to cooperate next time. Playlistening is not just fun in the present moment, it's also a proactive way to build cooperation and connection for the future.

Look back to your childhood

Do you remember a time when you got told off as a child by a parent or teacher? Perhaps you felt like laughing and tried to suppress your giggles so that you didn't get accused of being cheeky and get into even more trouble. Unfortunately, our teachers and parents didn't understand the importance of laughter. When we found it hard to keep our giggles under control, we were actually trying to use our natural healing process. We were trying to laugh away tension and find our way back to connection and cooperation; however, our parents or teachers probably set limits in a stern, serious way that didn't allow much space for us to release our feelings through laughter. We learnt to suppress our laughter, just like we did our tears. Gradually, we also suppressed some of our ability to play, make others laugh and have joyful fun with each other.

Our society operates to supress laughter in a similar way to how our tears are repressed. People get triggered by laughter because it unconsciously reminds them of all the times they wanted to laugh freely and joyfully but weren't able to. I recently visited a playgroup where a boy was shushed simply for laughing a lot. Even laughter can be viewed as a bad behaviour or something to get annoyed about.

Now, when we try to be playful, our own past hurts make it difficult. It can be hard to invest time or find the energy for play. We may even unconsciously supress our children's laughter without even realising it, as we sometimes do with tears.

Many parents label themselves as not playful or fun. This is often our past hurts talking. Humans are all born with an innately playful, joyful nature, but our experiences can suppress this side of ourselves.

We may struggle to come up with playlistening ideas to get our kids laughing. Or we might find that our children naturally set up situations to laugh and play, and want us to do something again and again, but we don't have the energy or stamina to keep going.

Play can be difficult because it triggers our own implicit memories of how adults played with us. In our present-day lives, we work hard and have lots of responsibilities. We don't always have much time for play and laughter.

Let listening time help you

It's really useful to do some listening time to explore our own thoughts, feelings and past stories about laughter and play. Who played with us when we were children? Did they make us laugh? Did they tickle? Did we feel safe or sometimes overwhelmed? How did the adults around us react to our laughter? During listening time we can also have a good old moan about how hard it is to play.

Mums sometimes struggle with laughter play and may think it's only for dads. Sometimes mums get overwhelmed by the more serious aspects of parenting and can't always find the room to laugh. Getting in touch with our own laughter can help us to discover that we all have a natural, playful self, whatever our age, gender or circumstances might be.

I was so fascinated by the power of laughter that I trained to be a laughter-yoga leader. The founder of laughter yoga, Madan Kataria, has said that before creating it he didn't feel like he had a very good sense of humour but that laughing regularly actually improved it.[2] It helped him get in touch with his natural humorous self.

Find a good listening partner that you can laugh with. Or meet up with a friend who has a great sense of humour. Watch a sitcom or some live comedy. When you practise listening time, and laugh with each other, you start exercising your own humour muscle. This can help you be naturally more playful with your children.

Through my laughter-yoga training I learnt all about the powerful effects of laughter on the body. Laughter raises endorphin levels and reduces our stress hormone levels. What's interesting is that fake laughter has all the physiological benefits of genuine laughter.

When I learnt this, I often tried to laugh along with my daughter, even if I didn't feel that good. I could 'fake it until I made it' and still get the health benefits and feel-good endorphins associated with a good giggle. If the day seemed long, and we were both a bit tired and grumpy, I could help to improve both our moods just by bringing in a bit of laughter.

Getting laughter flowing is an intuitive rather than an intellectual skill. If we start thinking about what will make our children laugh, our ideas may fall flat. Listening time is one way that we can tap into our intuitive, emotional, connecting side. We might also find that ideas naturally come to us when we are feeling better ourselves. Doing anything that fills you with joy can help.

If you are not sure how to start playlistening, it can be helpful to do some special time as a warm-up. When we follow our child's lead, doing what they like to do, we can tap into their world and might get more of an intuitive sense of what makes them laugh.

Alternatively, you could try relaxing and hanging out with your child, leaving the to-do list aside for a while. When we slow down, we can make time to be more joyful and playful. Laughter often automatically follows.

It'll all end in tears

Do you remember people saying, 'It'll all end in tears'? It is often said as a warning by adults when children get too exuberant and giggly. The adults in our lives may have shied away from playing too wildly with us as children, thinking that when we got too giggly we were out of control. Children will inevitably get a few bumps and bruises when they play a bit roughly, but as long as we set limits on anything dangerous or harmful to others or ourselves, we can keep playing, even as things get wilder and more giggly.

Sometimes, what happens is that a child will get a small bump and have a big cry about it, which is more about their emotions than a physical hurt. They've been laughing and having fun with us, and releasing stress and anxiety that have built up over time. This may trigger deeper hurts that children naturally let go of through crying. They sense our closeness and availability to listen to their upsets.

Often what's behind that warning is a fear not just of possible physical hurt but of emotional upset too. Adults might feel the urge to put a stop to any behaviour that gets too wild, or even too fun, because they want to keep their children safe from being hurt. There may also be an unconscious element of not wanting our children to display strong emotions.

Tears may often follow playlistening. It could be immediately afterwards, perhaps if we need to put a stop to the play for some reason, or a few hours later, when there is some kind of broken-cookie moment. I have noticed that if my daughter laughs a lot, there will almost always be a big cry brewing in the near future. If everything's well in the present, the tears are often just a natural part of the healing process. Laughter brings other emotions closer to the surface. Like rain after the sunshine, tears often follow.

It can seem strange to think that fun could cause our children to get upset. It doesn't make sense until we think of these tears not as a sign that something has gone wrong, but that they are positive, healthy and healing.

Experiencing the natural way our own emotions flow is often the best demonstration of what our children are going through. When we become more aware of our own emotions, we may start to notice that our own upsets happen after happy times, and they're not something negative or bad.

When I began laughter yoga, I learnt about doing continuous laughter meditation, which is basically laughing non-stop for a set period of time. The first time I tried it I remember feeling sad afterwards. I remembered that I hadn't phoned my sister for a long while and missed her because I was living abroad. The continuous laughter cleared out my mind to feel something that was important to me. After the tears, I felt happier, and I also decided to make the effort to call my sister. Fully feeling my emotions allowed me to live my life in a more enriching, authentic way.

We have all kinds of little hurts and worries hidden away, and we can make space for these emotions and embrace them. Then we can embrace our children's emotions, let their tears flow and realise it's all part of the process. Through laughing and crying we return to joy.

Case Study: David

'I was feeling really rejected by my son, because when I came home from work he wouldn't want to play with me, and I didn't know how to connect with him to get him playing. During a Hand in Hand Parenting workshop I talked about this in my listening time and the instructor asked me how my father played with me when I was young and if he wanted to play with me.

'I recalled how my father never played with me and that play was just for children, and how I felt really sad about his attitude. I talked about how I wanted things to be different with my own son. I realised that the pain of rejection I had when my son wouldn't play with me related to my father not wanting to play with me. I talked a lot about these feelings of rejection and cried a bit.

'Then the instructor helped me to see how I could do reconnecting play with my son. I would take a doll and talk to it, saying things like, "Did you just see that? He doesn't want to play with me!" I acted out my rejection in a playful way. Then I would say in the voice of the doll, "Yes of course, because you haven't been home all day, and you didn't call today."

'Then in the voice of the doll I would ask my son, "How about now? Will you play with your dad?" My son would say no, and got to feel powerful. I would pretend to cry, and my son would laugh. After playing these games for a while we could happily reconnect after my day apart from him at work.'

EXERCISE: Reflection – Having fun in your past and now

1   Who played with you as a child?

2   Who do you enjoy laughing with – someone from your past or the present?

2   Phone a friend or call a listening partner with whom you laugh a lot.

3   How could you bring more laughter into your life?

4   What fills you with joy? Write a 'loving life' to-do list and work your way through it.

EXERCISE: Try this: playlistening games

This is a rough guide to what might make your child laugh. Use these games as a starting point, and follow wherever the giggles lead you.

- **Peek-a-boo** This traditional game of hiding and reappearing helps your child with feelings about separation.

- **Bouncing babies** Bounce your baby on your lap, while sitting somewhere soft like a bed or sofa, then very gently let them fall off your lap and onto the bed, and say 'Oops!' if they laugh and like it. Be careful to watch for cues that they are enjoying it, and stop if they aren't.

- **Stack of toys** Try to put toys in a stack and then let them fall down. Exclaim 'Oops!' and act exasperated and frustrated when they fall.

- **Tower of bricks** Make a tower of bricks, and make a big deal about how proud you are of your wonderful tower. Then walk away saying 'I hope nobody knocks my tower down', which will be a sure invitation for your toddler to knock it down! Exclaim 'Oh no!' and act befuddled, in a mock-frustrated way saying, 'What happened to my tower?!'

- **Parcel for the Post Office** This is a good one to try if your toddler is clingy and sitting in your lap. Pretend she is a parcel that you need to wrap up and take to the Post Office. Pretend to wrap her up, and then say, 'Oh, this parcel keeps moving', or 'This parcel isn't sitting straight', inviting them to be in the more powerful role, and wriggle and slouch, as you try to wrap your parcel. Then you might want to put the parcel by the door and say something like, 'I'll just put my parcel there ready for the Post Office; I hope it doesn't

▶

move.' Then, when the parcel moves, act all mock-frustrated and cross.

- **Making the bed** You might find that making beds automatically becomes an opportunity for playlistening as your child tries to crawl under the sheets or jump on the bed, and disrupt the process. Start making a bed when you have plenty of time to be in fun mode, and invite them to play, saying, 'I hope nobody crawls under the sheets.' Then you might feel around saying something like, 'Oh dear, there seem to be bobbles under this sheet, I need to flatten them down', and do so in a playful way that gets them laughing.

- **Swing giggles** When you are pushing your baby or toddler in a swing, pretend to fall over as the swing approaches, or tell them 'I hope you don't kick me', inviting them to kick you as the swing approaches, then fall over. Contrary to popular belief, games like this actually reduce aggression because feelings can be channelled in a playful, safe context. In a similar way cats, dogs and other mammals will playfight with their parents or siblings without inflicting actual injury, because there is an instinctual understanding of the difference between when something is a game and when it is serious.

- **Walking and falling** When toddlers are learning to walk, they often find it funny to watch us walk off and then fall down, over and over again.

- **Jumping champion** This is great for a child who is learning to jump or is frustrated by their physical abilities. Tell your toddler that you are the jumping champion, and can do the biggest jumps in the world. Then try to jump and only do a tiny jump, or jump and then fall over.

▶

- **Objects in a bag** Tell your child that you need to pack a bag. Put some objects in a small bag, but keep letting them fall out. Act surprised that it's not working, and pretend to get angry and frustrated.

- **Winning race** This game is great for toddlers that are starting to feel competitive with others. Tell your toddler that you are going to have a running competition to see who gets there first. Let him win, and then exclaim, 'I can't believe you won! I was trying so hard!'

- **Me first** Tell your child that you are going to be first to open the door, press the lift button, go to the toilet, and so on. Make a big thing of turning it into a competition, and then let her win. This is perfect for competitive siblings.

- **Getting the words wrong** When you need to talk to your toddler, try getting the words wrong, and then say, 'Oh no! That's not right, that's not the word I was trying to say, I was trying to say . . .' Keep trying to say a certain word and keep getting it wrong. You can do the same when you are reading a storybook, where you suddenly come out with the wrong word and act surprised. This game is great for releasing any tension around language learning, and also helps your child relax before sleep.

CHAPTER 12

Behaviour – Building Cooperation Through Connection

•

'A limit set gently and with love is a gift
that builds connection.'

Patty Wipfler

When I first learnt about the concept of peaceful or gentle parenting, one question was stuck in my mind. I could understand the concept of doing our best to be nice to our children, but what if they did something wrong, or what if I needed to make them do something? How exactly do you make children do what you want them to do? Wouldn't they be out of control if you were just nice to them the whole time?

As our babies turn into toddlers, we may be dreading the 'terrible twos' or the 'threenager' year. I remember going on a hectic trip to see family at Christmas when my daughter was 18 months old, and when we returned she started fighting me about everything: getting dressed, going into her buggy, having her nappy changed. It seemed as if she had turned into a toddler overnight!

As I began to spend more quality time with her, doing special time and playlistening, and listening to the upsets that bubbled up, all her off-track behaviour melted away. I realised that what

I thought were the terrible twos was in fact a natural reaction to stress and change.

In the end, the terrible twos never came. There were phases where I needed to give my daughter more attention, and listen to her feelings; there were phases when I was exhausted or stressed and couldn't connect with her very well, and I would often see that reflected in her behaviour. But we could overcome all this using the Hand in Hand Parenting tools.

Helping our child through setting limits

In reality, we don't actually have to make our children do anything. Our children actually don't want to spend their lives struggling and fighting against us. They don't want to make our life hard. But they do want to tell us about their feelings.

It's feelings that get in the way of our child's ability to think well and listen to our reasoning about why it's a good idea to do or not do certain things. As we have seen, when we connect and listen to our children's feelings, their off-track behaviour will reduce and we'll see their natural cooperative nature shining through.

When feelings aren't clouding our child's thinking we can usually come to a consensus together. Our children can respect our needs and wishes too, and often have good judgement about what they want and need.

When upset feelings are making them behave in off-track ways, we need to set limits to stop the behaviour and also to help them with their emotions. When we are in a situation where we think we need to set a limit, we should first assess the situation to see if they are really off-track or just behaving in a way that is normal or natural for their age.

Does a limit really need to be set?

Babies and toddlers love to play and explore, and will get frustrated when we set too many limits on their discoveries. We can try to give them as much freedom as they need to explore in a safe environment. By doing so we build their trust and cooperation. They understand that we have their best interests at heart. When they have the freedom to play and explore, as well as having their feelings listened to, they will be more likely to be flexible and understand when we need to stop them from touching something unsafe.

There are other possible situations where we might jump to the conclusion that our child is off-track when in fact their behaviour comes from a genuine need rather than from upset feelings; for example, if our child is running around the apartment for fun, this might not be an off-track behaviour that we need to set a limit and stop but more of a need for exercise and play. If we're worried about disturbing the neighbours, taking them outside to run around might be a good compromise.

If we want our child to hug a relative, this might also not be an appropriate moment to set a limit, because when it comes to giving affection it's important that our children have a say in when and if they give some. Our child's behaviour probably isn't off-track, but she might be doing something that is natural for their age. In cases like these we don't need to set a limit on our child's behaviour but rather to find a way to meet her need.

Setting limits: the connected way

With Hand in Hand Parenting we set limits on behaviour whenever we notice that our child is off-track; for example, when they are about to hit another toddler, throw a toy or take a toy off another child, or if we need to change his nappy, or we have to leave the house, and he refuses.

As explained in Chapter 3, when we need to set a limit, we should move in closely, get down to our child's level and look at him. With young children who are acting off-track and can't think straight, we need to physically show the limit, as well as just telling them that they can't hit their friend or throw a toy. Our words won't be enough, because when they're upset, the pre-frontal cortex (the language part of the brain) isn't functioning well. We could gently take hold of their hand or the toy and say, 'I'm sorry, I can't let you throw this.'

Moving in close means our child has a sense of connection to us while we set the limit. What often happens is that when our child feels our presence, he might release whatever emotion was behind the behaviour. He might start crying or laughing. In a sense the limit we bring becomes his broken-cookie moment that helps him to release his feelings.

As with any other time we listen to our children, we set limits slowly so that they sense we are there and available to listen to them. If our toddler is about to hit another with a toy, for example, we could take hold of the toy and her hand, and tell her, 'I can't let you have this now.'

We should allow them to express whatever they are feeling in the moment, rather than just immediately grabbing the toy out of their hand and walking off. That way we are making a connection and giving them the opportunity to release their feelings.

As we slowly keep hold of the toy they wanted to throw, they might struggle to grab it back and start to cry. We can keep hold of the toy, and keep the limit, but listen and empathise with the feelings as we would do at any other time when they are upset.

Our child knows we are always there for them

Giving attention and warmth doesn't mean that we condone the behaviour but that we understand that our child doesn't want to hurt others and that their actions are caused by upset feelings. This is a wonderful gift to our child, a big dose of unconditional love, that no matter how they feel we will always be there for them. They feel fully accepted without shame or blame. They can then let go of their feelings so that they don't need to tell us about them through their behaviour.

Setting limits like this, staying in the moment, means we don't need to use physical force to drag our child out of the house or to take off his nappy against his will. It's respectful and empowering for children to have their feelings heard. What's amazing is that after setting limits our child can think clearly, and if the request was reasonable he can understand our thinking.

Why this is not 'permissive' parenting

Often gentle parenting, or peaceful parenting, is thought of as 'permissive parenting'. It's assumed that being nice to children all the time means letting them do whatever they want; however, permissive parenting is not in the best interests of the child, because if we ignore their off-track behaviour then we are ultimately ignoring their emotions too.

With Hand in Hand Parenting we set limits early, as soon as we get the slightest indication that our child is acting off-track and isn't feeling good. This is for two reasons. One, it means that we stop the behaviour before we get more irritated and lose our patience for listening. Two, it means that our child doesn't have to carry her upset feelings for any longer than is necessary.

If our child is moany and whiny, we don't wait all day until she starts destroying the house or pulling the cat's tail, or hurting her brother over and over again until we are exhausted and exasperated. If we notice our child is slightly off-track, we can move in closely and connect with her to help her with her feelings. If we notice our child woke up grumpy and is asking for her breakfast with a desperate tone, and we suspect that there are upset feelings behind the mood, we can listen to these feelings before we get the food. We can get down to her level, give her a hug and say, 'I'll get you your breakfast in a minute.' Just having us close might trigger all the feelings behind the whinyness so that she has the space to get them out, and they don't interfere with the rest of the day.

This is a proactive way of noticing that our child isn't feeling good and showing that we are available to listen to her feelings. If we rushed around trying to get breakfast ready without giving her a few minutes of connection, our child's feelings wouldn't be addressed. We could let the moanyness and whinyness slide, and avoid being there to set a gentle limit and offer some connection. But ultimately this doesn't help either of us in the long run. If we ignore our child's smaller red flags – the ways they tell us they need our connection – she will need to resort to more extreme behaviour to grab our attention. Being there whenever our children 'ask' us for attention stops the behaviour, and also makes it much less likely to happen in the future.

Setting limits with laughter

Sometimes, when we move in close and set a limit, our child begins laughing. This is a sure sign that his feelings are more of the lighter, giggly type, and we can playfully set limits so that he can release them. As discussed in the previous chapter, laughter can help to build the connection children need in order to cooperate.

Perhaps our child opens a kitchen cupboard and takes out a packet of rice, then starts pouring it on the floor. If they are younger, it might be about play and exploration, but if they're older and have an awareness of what rice is actually for, it's probably more to do with wanting our attention and connection.

We could playfully grab their hands and say, 'No, no, no', with a warm friendly tone, and a smile on our face. They might try pulling the rice away from us, while laughing. As we are both holding on to the rice, playing a push-and-pull game, they are absorbing all of our warm connection and can sense that we accept their feelings without shame or blame.

Or we could put the rice away in the cupboard, take our child's hand and walk away saying, in a playful tone, 'I hope no one takes the rice out of the cupboard again.' Your child may just take this as an invitation to play, and wriggle away and run back to the cupboard, where you can follow them and start to set a limit again. In the short term this looks like we are encouraging the behaviour, turning it into a game, which will only make our child want to play at overstepping this limit again and again; however, while we play this game, we allow our child to show us the ways in which they are feeling off-track. They get to soak up our warm attention. If we have the patience to play and connect through the game, it means that our child will actually be less likely to 'misbehave' in the future because they have been given the attention they were seeking.

When we need to actually set a limit (rather than simply playing) we can also physically show the limit, so that our child gets to play and laugh while we are in control of holding the limit; for example, in this scenario, you might take your child's hand and say playfully, 'Come on, let's go away from the cupboard.' And then say quietly to yourself, 'I hope you don't run away and try to get the rice back.' As they playfully run away, you can reach the cupboard just in time, and be there to make sure it stays shut, and then repeat the game again. This way it's clear that there is a limit, but that you are playing around it.

We could just leave the rice out, and let them play with it, but we might not want to waste the rice. It also does not serve our child very well. If they are doing something in an attempt to grab our attention, if we just give in and say yes to them, we are permissively giving them what they 'want' while not paying attention to the underlying 'need' that is manifest in their off-track behaviour.

Be consistent with playful limit-setting

At first glance it can seem that setting limits with laughter isn't a very effective tool. After all, our child just wants to turn it into a game and may have the stamina to play for a long time before agreeing with what we want.

For most of us it's a big leap, to actually encourage the behaviour we are setting out to stop. We have to make sure that it is a behaviour that we have the patience to be playful about, and that we set limits in such a way that we stop any real damage or harm from being done. If we stop our child from hitting her brother, by playfully catching her hand, then we have to make sure that we playfully catch her hands each and every time she tries to hit so that everyone is safe. We should explain that we can't let her hit her brother. After a while the situation is not so charged full of feelings and our child will probably just move on to doing something else, feeling more connected to us, and with less of a need to try to grab our attention with her behaviour.

If you have only just started using the Hand in Hand Parenting approach, your child might need to laugh and play a lot. You might see more off-track behaviour for a while, as they sense that you are available to playlisten and they can bring up their backlog of feelings to play with and heal.

As you allow your child to be playfully off-track, with limits on anything that is unacceptable, or bring playlistening and special time into their lives, they will be able to work through their feelings and this will reduce the likelihood of future off-track behaviour.

Connecting to our child is essential

As we learn and discover how to use the Hand in Hand Parenting tools we'll get a sense of whether we need to use play and laughter or empathetic listening. It's just a matter of tuning into our child and sensing how they are feeling, and what kind of connection they need from us in the moment.

Sometimes we might find that we set a limit and no feelings come up at all. This could be for a number of reasons. It might be that we're not getting down to their level, giving them eye contact and really offering our connection when we set limits. I know I often get caught up with life and forget to be fully present with my daughter, and so it's good to remind ourselves to be fully there when we need to set a limit.

It could also be that our child is feeling particularly disconnected from us and might need more special time or play to feel our presence strongly enough to release their feelings. It could also be that we've had to set a lot of limits with them recently and we need to rebalance the power dynamic by giving them more freedom.

Sometimes our child might sense that we are not really present or connected enough to listen to them because we're not feeling good ourselves and we aren't in the right frame of mind to listen. We can set an intention to get some listening time as soon as possible, to release our own feelings so that we can be the calm listener that our child needs.

A general rule for Hand in Hand Parenting is that if one tool isn't working, trying another will help the situation.

Maintain a balance between freedom and limit setting

Children need a sense of freedom, agency to explore, play and enjoy life. We may sometimes go through phases where we've felt it was necessary to set a lot of limits. If so, we should be careful to balance this out with an extra injection of play and special time. Our children need warm connection and lots of confirmation from us to counteract the times we need to say no.

We should also give our child plenty of freedom to make decisions about what goes on in their lives. What we will find is that when toddlers get listened to regularly, they have quite a clear idea of their wants and needs; for example, when they say no to a bath, sometimes it can be that it's a broken-cookie moment and they are saying no because some fears and upsets are being triggered and they don't know how to express them other than saying no to us. On the other hand, it could be that they actually just don't feel like having a bath, and feel really tired, and would rather just cuddle up with a story.

As we learn and discover using these tools and staying close to our children we can work out when they are off-track or when they're saying no to something they actually don't want to do.

Using listening time for exploring setting limits

Setting limits in a way that is warm, loving and unconditionally accepting of our children is incredibly challenging. It's definitely one of the hardest aspects of one of the hardest jobs in the world!

Few of us had experiences of our own parents setting limits with warmth. Our parents may have reacted in a stern and serious way. In the past, experts weren't aware of the brain science that shows that children find it difficult to control their behaviour when they're feeling upset. We might have been shouted at or blamed and shamed for our behaviour. We may have been physically hurt, or sent to our rooms. We probably didn't have parents who empathised and understood why we acted in that way.

We are born with this natural healing process and may have instinctively tried to use it by starting to laugh or cry when our parents set limits for us. Our parents probably didn't respond with much empathy. They may have seen our outbursts as disobedience or manipulation. Laughter would have been seen as being cheeky or disrespectful.

Because our parents didn't understand the healing power of tears, or have the emotional resources to listen to us, they probably withdrew warmth and connection in order to avoid our feelings when they set limits.

As well as the upset feelings, we also had further upset piled on to us from our parents' reactions to our behaviour, and to our attempts to heal. We would tend to withdraw our feelings and give up on trying to tell them how we felt. This is an enormous burden to carry through life, and it all gets triggered when our children are off-track. We simultaneously have to deal with their behaviour and our own past story. It's no wonder we feel stressed and irritable.

Off-track behaviour can really push our buttons. When our child whines and moans it brings up all our childhood stuff. There are voices in our head saying things like, 'Stop whining', 'Don't make such a fuss' or 'Don't cry or I'll give you something to cry about.'

We can use listening time to deal with our frustration, to get out all the things we feel like saying or doing to our children when they act off-track. Then, next time, our head will be clearer to respond with warmth.

It's good to remember that there is a positive side to experiencing our child's off-track behaviour. All of our child's feelings that may seem buried and hidden at times are actually right there being acted out. Behaviour is like a key for unlocking our child's feelings so that they can feel better.

It's also good to remember that whatever is going on with your child, there is nothing wrong with them. The acting out is not part of their intrinsic nature but a display of how they are feeling. Feelings can change.

It's helpful to use listening time or just think about some of the preconceptions we might have around limit setting and crying, since these often come from our own childhood experiences; for example, the idea that children cry when we set limits in order to try to get us to back down.

Children who are listened to don't need to manipulate

Children who are listened to will rarely use tears to manipulate and get what they want. This only happens if children sense that we're afraid of their tears, and would do anything to stop them.

When we parent by connection, our children won't experience us giving in to avoid their tears. They won't sense that we are afraid of tears and that they can use them as a way to gain power and control over us. They'll also experience what it is to have genuine power over their lives so that they won't need to seek it out in more manipulative ways.

A frequently held view is that children use tears to get what they want, and this is one of the ways our society encourages us to avoid and withdraw attention from tears. In many situations we'll find that children aren't using tears to get what they want but simply to express their emotions; for example, I remember once I was babysitting a five-year-old boy at his house and the doorbell rang. A friend of his wanted to come inside to play, but we were just getting ready to go out to his music class. When I told the boy he couldn't invite his friend in he immediately started to cry. At first I thought that he was crying to get me to allow his friend to come in, and I was a bit nervous at the way he was testing my authority. Then I noticed him walking away from the door, and realised that he wasn't crying to try to gain power over me. He was crying even as he accepted the limit I had set. He just needed to let go of some of his disappointment.

We need to remind ourselves that our children are born wanting to express their feelings to us. When it appears that they are manipulating or playing us, it's often that they are asking for opportunities not to get what they want but to express their feelings.

Quick-fix setting limits – for when we can't listen

We need to recognise when we don't have the patience to set limits in a warm, connecting way. In these cases, we can try to set limits in a way that protects our family and keeps them safe, but without listening to the feelings. We can take time to sit down and take some deep breaths ourselves and make an intention to get listening time later.

Setting limits with warmth might take longer than the immediate compliance that adults sometimes expect from children. Our children might need to cry for a while, or they might want to laugh and play before they are free of feelings and can think clearly and accept that our limit is reasonable. As we bring the Hand in Hand Parenting tools into our lives more regularly, our children will lighten their emotional load, so setting limits will take less time and we won't need to set limits so often because more and more often we'll see their natural cooperative nature shining through.

Listening time allows us to heal along with our children. All those buttons our children push are little places of hurt that we've been carrying. We can let go of those hurts and grow too.

Case Study: Astrid

'I went to the supermarket with my children and a friend, and they were all begging for sweets. I decided that this time I would get some for everybody to share. They were all happy with a few sweets each, but my younger daughter wasn't. She kept saying she wanted one more. I told her that she couldn't have any more. She grabbed the sweets away from me. I put my hand on her hand with the sweets, and said, "No, I'm sorry, you can't have any more sweets. That was enough." She started screaming and I just kept telling her that I was sorry that she couldn't have any more.

'I didn't just grab the sweets away. That's something I learnt from Hand in Hand Parenting. Before, I would have just grabbed the packet and walked away from her. The funny thing was my daughter wasn't grabbing the packet and pulling it away either. I really felt that what she wanted more than the sweets was to connect with me.

'She kept crying. After ten minutes of crying with both of our hands on the sweets, she started to say through her tears, "You go away with Tim, you go away with Tim!" Then I realised what the crying was about. In two days I would be leaving with her brother to go away on a weekend just for the two of us, for a long special time, and she was jealous and upset about it. I explained that yes, I was going to go away with Tim, and that we needed that time to reconnect, but that another time she and I could have a long special time together too. She cried for a bit longer and then let me take the sweets away.

'That's the amazing thing about setting limits; although my daughter seemed to be crying about sweets she was actually pouring out other emotions about separation from me. When I left for the weekend with Tim she said goodbye, and she said happily, 'I know mummy's coming back.' I was so glad I was able to set a limit about the sweets, as I could leave her knowing she was OK with it.'

EXERCISE: Reflection – behaviour that you find irritating

1   What is your child's most irritating behaviour? Have a good moan about it. How would your parents have reacted if you showed this kind of behaviour when you were a child?

2   What methods did your parents use to set limits with you? Do you think they were effective?

CHAPTER 13

Sleep – Transform Your Parenting with Eight Hours a Night

•

'A good laugh and a long sleep are the best cures
in the doctor's book.'

Irish proverb

Which of your parenting challenges would be solved if everyone in your family could get a good night's sleep? When I speak to parents who say they've lost patience or they can't be the parents they want to be, it's often because they are feeling stressed and exhausted from lack of sleep. Stress and exhaustion make it more likely that our limbic system becomes overwhelmed with emotion so that our pre-frontal cortex stops functioning well and it becomes harder to parent in a way that we feel good about.

It's a little known fact that babies and toddlers often find it hard to fall asleep or wake when they are feeling stressed and upset for the same reason that adults do.[1] We don't automatically consider this reason, because most of the parenting information about infant and toddler sleep focuses on creating a stable routine, but it doesn't often address their emotional needs.

Babies and toddlers experience sleep as a time of separation. Using the Hand in Hand Parenting tools helps them to release the feelings that get in the way of having a strong connection to us. When they have fewer upset feelings, they might automatically start sleeping better. Following the steps in this book means that you are already on the way to having a good night's sleep. In this chapter I'll share some information on how to help children fall asleep and sleep through the night without their feelings getting in the way.

Falling asleep with babies

With babies, you might notice in the evening that there's a time when they're getting grumpy and nothing pleases them. This can be a sign that they need to cry to release their feelings, although we might not realise it.

I used to keep trying to feed my daughter and she would keep coming off the breast. I tried lots of different methods to get her to stop crying, including continuing to try to feed her and pacing the house while carrying her.

The big newsflash about sleep is that we often unknowingly create our children's sleep problems, and we start doing this during babyhood. We were never taught that babies and children need to cry regularly to release their emotions, and that they will often choose the time before sleep to do so.

When our babies cry in the evening, we may go to extraordinary lengths to stop the crying, thinking that we are helping them sleep. We may bounce or rock them for long periods, or even drive them around for hours. Eventually, our babies will fall asleep, but we may notice that as time goes on it gets harder and harder and takes longer and longer. They may also wake in the night.

The big confusion we have around sleep is that we assume that babies cry because they are tired and need our help to sleep. Actually, their crying in our presence is often something they are doing to help them get to sleep. Babies will instinctively let go of feelings before naptime or at the end of the day so that they sleep well.

With young babies, feeding and sleep sometimes coincide. We'll be getting used to our baby and their rhythm and needs. As they get older we'll be able to work out more easily what they need and will know the difference between when they are hungry and when they are tired. If we listen closely to what they need and notice when they simply have a need to cry, we can help them to release the feelings so that they can naturally regulate their emotions and sleep easily and deeply in the way nature intended.

Using stillness to fall asleep

When my daughter was about six months old I began to realise that I was always doing something to her to help her sleep. Whether it was carrying her in a sling, or trying multiple times to feed her, or putting her in her pram and going for a walk, or bouncing her. I was never simply allowing her to simply fall asleep without some kind of prop.

Babies, just like adults, can fall asleep simply by closing their eyes when they are tired and falling asleep. They don't actually need us to do anything to get them to sleep. They just need us to be there, so that they feel safe and connected. The major difference, though, is that babies have feelings very close to the surface. They are still getting used to being in the world and haven't learnt the adult patterns of holding their feelings in, so when the world is new and incredibly stimulating, they will naturally cry before falling asleep.

When I was questioning the healing power of tears, wondering whether it was really right to just let my daughter cry, I remembered how when I first started yoga and meditation I was surprised to find that the practice of being still didn't always bring me the calm I expected. It often brought uncomfortable emotions to the surface. Over time, I realised that this stillness allowed dormant emotions to rise to the surface of my mind so that I could release them. There were hurts and pains that I hadn't been conscious of, that I let go of to feel at peace. Later I would write about how I was feeling and I would often cry, but I always felt better for having had that stillness to clear out the stagnant emotions. I now realise that I was crying, writing and making sense of things to get a greater sense of peace – through this I was making a coherent story. I wasn't aware of those emotions, but it was still baggage that I carried. These emotions would be triggered by everyday situations that were hard to cope with because of that unconscious baggage.

I realised that if I was always doing something to help my daughter to sleep, she wouldn't get to experience that stillness. I then started holding her in my arms before sleep, as long as I was sure that she didn't need anything. I was amazed that she would sometimes fall asleep with a big smile on her face, or even laughing. When we sit and just be present with our children, whether it's offering special time or playing, or holding them in our arms before sleep, we are offering that stillness, a place where they can simply be, and we can notice what they are feeling. Sometimes, especially when they are young, they may cry.

If your baby gets upset before sleep, run through your checklist of needs just like you would at any other time. Are they still hungry, tired, hot or cold? Could there be a medical reason why they're upset? If we're sure that all their needs are met, we should remember to notice if we are doing something simply to stop the crying rather than meeting a need. We don't need to rock or bounce our baby, or drive our baby around for hours – or any of the other myriad ways we parents use to get our babies to sleep. We might find that if we're out and about, our babies naturally fall asleep with movement in a sling or a buggy, but it's worth balancing this out with time spent falling asleep at home, so that they have a chance to be listened to. We can sit and hold them and just be with them, and tell them that they're safe, and that we'll listen as long as they are upset.

As time goes by, your baby will get used to being in the world. She will release any stress that has accumulated from pregnancy or her birth, or other difficult experiences. She will cry less and less before sleep, and be more likely to sleep deeply, and for longer, naturally without ever needing to be left alone to cry it out.

Giggling to sleep

With older babies or toddlers you might have noticed that in the evening it seems like there's a 'giggle hour' where your child gets really giggly and wants to run, laugh and play. This is also part of the way children naturally regulate their emotions in order to sleep well. The tension of the day can be laughed and played away, so that relaxation easily follows.

My daughter used to do something her dad called the 'pyjama run', which was whenever she saw us pick up her pyjamas in the evening she would immediately start crawling or running away. At the end of the day we are tired and often desperate for some time alone, but it's really helpful if you can go along with the play. This way we can help children find their genuine tiredness and the strong sense of connection that they need in order to sleep well. It works much better than forcing them into bed before they are ready, and then feeling frustrated when they don't fall asleep. When children start getting regular doses of play like this they won't need to do it for so long every single time.

A lot of the parenting advice for sleep focuses on babies and toddlers having a calm routine. Many parents assume that we shouldn't try to 'wind children up' at the end of the day, and that we have to keep things slow and quiet to get them ready to sleep. This is actually incorrect, because laughter is, in fact, clinically proven to be a great sleep inducer. In one study, breastfeeding women were divided into two groups. One group watched a

Charlie Chaplin film to get them laughing, while a control group didn't watch it. The researchers measured the amount of melatonin – a hormone released by the brain at the onset of sleep, in the breast milk of each group of women and found that those who watched the film had more melatonin.[2] So laughter really is the best sleeping pill around!

A bedtime rhythm

Instead of a strict routine it's better to have a rhythm to our evening that allows plenty of space for feelings and for our child to find his natural tiredness. We can sprinkle giggles throughout our bedtime routine whenever we can find a playlistening opportunity. You might want to add ten minutes of rough-and-tumble before getting into pyjamas and bed, particularly if your child seems to have some leftover energy from the day. Slowing down the bedtime routine to make it more connected will actually speed up the falling asleep process because your child will be more relaxed.

Children might indicate to us when they are feeling disconnected and where they need an extra dose of connection before going to sleep, such as refusing to clean their teeth, put on pyjamas or have a bath. When we need to set limits on teeth cleaning or bath time, we can try to find ways to make these moments playful. Perhaps the rubber ducks beg our toddler to get in the bath, or the toothbrush is an aeroplane that needs to land in their mouth.

We might find that there are times when our child starts to cry. Perhaps they get upset about teeth cleaning, or frustrated because they are trying to put on their pyjamas and they are all tangled up. It's important that we take our time and don't force clothes on or clean teeth against our child's will. Babies and toddlers often attach fears to bath time or teeth cleaning because they can seem strange and unusual when they're young.

It's really helpful if we can listen and offer cuddles when they're upset, to slowly show them the toothbrush or the water, and to slowly set a limit, to give them all the time they need to release their fears and upsets.

We might assume our child is overtired and distract them from their feelings, then rush through the night-time routine to try to get them to sleep. This can be counterproductive because they need to release the stress and upset to sleep well. It's better to listen, even if we know that deep down our child is exhausted, because helping them release their feelings means they'll sleep better for that night and in the longer term.

If our child often takes a long time to fall asleep, and we are sure they must be tired, often it's because there's something on their mind that means it's hard to relax. Some last-minute laughter is frequently what they need to give them the connection and relaxation they need to fall asleep. Perhaps we can read them one more bedtime story using a funny voice or getting the words wrong in places and then saying, 'Oh no! That's not right!' Or perhaps we get all serious and put a stuffed toy to bed pretending we think it's our child, and exclaim with surprise when we realise our mistake.

Night wakings and night weaning

Most parenting approaches to night waking fall into two areas. On the one hand there is a hard way that involves sleep training – leaving a baby alone to cry, so they get trained to understand that a parent won't respond to them in the night. The problem with this approach is that it doesn't address the baby's or toddler's need for connection and closeness. Whatever the age, when they are upset they need someone there to listen to their feelings. Babies stop calling out because they learn that their parents won't respond. They might learn to sleep well, but their feelings might come out in more indirect ways like off-track behaviour. Later on, sleep issues might arise again such as a fear of the dark or nightmares.

The second kind of approach is where a parent always responds to a baby or toddler and accepts that it's natural that they wake frequently. With this approach we might feed them when they ask for it, rock them back to sleep, give them a dummy or arrange their blanket in the exact way they like it. This approach is gentle and supportive of the child because we don't leave them alone, but it also isn't in the best interests of the child. The trouble with this approach is that often the surface need of wanting to feed for comfort or sleep with a dummy in their mouth masks a deeper need to cry. We might notice that our child's sleep doesn't improve at all as they get older. They might continue to wake night after night. Sleep might even get worse as they accumulate a backlog of feelings.

It is common for older babies and toddlers to wake up at night, but that is because the healing power of tears isn't well understood. Older babies and toddlers, who haven't had the chance to let go of emotions from their upsetting experiences, will wake frequently.

There is a third way that involves noticing if there is an underlying emotional need behind the waking. If we suspect that there isn't really a need other than the need to express feelings, then the kindest and most beneficial thing for our child is to allow them the chance to be listened to. Sometimes this might involve setting limits, for example, on feeding in the night, if we are sure our child is not actually hungry and that this surface need is masking the deeper need to cry.

According to Aletha Solter, healthy babies over the age of six months are able to sleep through the night. I would take this as a very rough guideline, because we are the best experts on our babies, and only we can tell if they can manage feeding less in the night, and when we feel ready and have enough resources to listen and feel comfortable about the process. There is also some research that says that feeding babies in the night and co-sleeping can reduce the risk of sudden infant death syndrome (SIDS).[3]

Night weaning peacefully

If you are ready to night wean your baby, you can do so gradually. Choose a weekend, if possible, or a time when you can sleep in, or ask a partner to help out.

It's essential to night wean gradually, so that your baby gets used to having less milk in the night and she might need to readjust her feeding, so that she drinks more in the day. Starting with the first waking each night, you can tell your baby that you aren't going to feed her but will be there to listen to her. Then if she wakes again later in the night, you can feed her as you normally do. This ensures that the process is gradual and your baby has time to get used to the change. You will find that over time the first waking becomes later and later, as she has fewer feelings waking her up and can sleep for longer periods. Soon she'll start sleeping through the night.

When I night-weaned my daughter I actually found that I felt so much closer to her when I helped her with the feelings that were causing her to wake rather than automatically breastfeeding her. I could hug her or hold her as she fell back to sleep, listening to whatever feelings arose, and I felt I was meeting her need on a much deeper level than simply feeding her.

We can take the night-weaning process slowly and listen little by little. If our child cries for a long time and we then decide to feed her, that's OK. There is no need to worry about being consistent. Our aim is not to form a habit or teach our baby that we won't respond in the night. Instead, we are listening, little by little, until she is able to release all the feelings that cause her to wake in the night.

If one night we just want to take a break and sleep as much as possible, that's OK. Every bit of listening helps, and the important thing to remember is that we need to be a calm, patient listener, and if we're exhausted ourselves, sometimes the best thing to do is to feed our baby and then go back to sleep. Each time we listen to a chunk of feelings, they will be less in the way of our child's ability to sleep peacefully through the night.

Early waking

Waking early can also be a sign that your child has feelings they need to release. With babies, we can sometimes mistake their waking early as hunger; however, if they are an older baby in a persistent pattern of waking early but are never really that hungry, it could be that feelings are causing them to wake up. This is often the case if they fall back to sleep straight after feeding. Or they stay awake but seem grumpy. We might attribute that to lack of sleep. It could be just an indication of the upset feelings that caused them to wake. If they're an older baby or toddler, and we're sure they're not hungry, we can try listening instead.

With toddlers, we might get more of a clue as to why your child has woken early. With my daughter, she sometimes woke early when she started a new playgroup or when we were travelling and staying in different places. Toddlers that wake early might start crying or become agitated and grumpy. Often it's not the tiredness per se that is causing the upset but the upset itself that caused the early waking, so we can simply staylisten whenever they're upset so that they will be more likely to sleep better the next night and in the future.

Sleeping arrangements

The Hand in Hand Parenting tools can help you find the sleeping arrangement that is best for your family. Before six months of age it's recommended that babies sleep in the same room as their parents.[4] Co-sleeping is a lovely way to connect and feel close to each other, but it's not the only way. With Hand in Hand Parenting we deepen the emotional sense of security our child has, so an older baby or toddler might feel completely happy sleeping in a separate bed or a separate room. They have internalised a sense of connection to us and know we are always there for them, wherever they sleep. If an older child has trouble falling asleep alone, this can sometimes be because separation anxiety gets triggered. Sometimes setting a limit and staylistening, while gradually leaving, as we discuss in Chapter 14, can help children feel safe to fall asleep alone.

Listening time to work through sleep issues

Sleep is complicated for many of us. We may have been left to cry it out as babies. We might have been night-weaned before we were ready. We might have been left alone to fall asleep even when we were full of feelings and really needed someone to listen to us.

Sometimes we get confused about what to do regarding our child's sleep, and the root of this confusion is often the hurt feelings we carry regarding how we were treated. We also experience other strong feelings such as desperation for our children to fall asleep quickly because we need a break from parenting.

Of course, listening time is the tool that can help us process these feelings. We can express some of our desperation and confusion, and trace its roots back to our own childhood experiences. We can talk about how sleep was for us as children, then it will become easier to help our children with their sleep issues.

If you suffer from sleep difficulties yourself, listening partnerships can help you release tension and sleep better. Our present-day sleep issues can be rooted in the past and our early experience around sleep, so talking about our memories around sleep and bedtime, or speculating about what sleep was like for us when we were a baby, can really help. If you wake up a lot in the night, a listening partner in a different time zone can be a great help! Writing down your thoughts when you wake up can also be beneficial. In a laboratory study, participants who wrote their thoughts on waking started sleeping better.[5]

Good sleep is so essential to ourselves and our children, and helping them to sleep through is something we can do for the well-being of our whole family. There will still be times when they might wake, perhaps during periods of emotional upheaval or illness, but on the whole, children who get listened to sleep much better.

Case Study: Hannah

'My son was three years old and he'd always co-slept with me and my husband. I didn't really mind him sleeping with us but I sensed that he had some separation fears that made it hard for him to sleep in his own bed. He had his own room with his own bed and I decided that I would start an 'emotional project' to try to get him to sleep in it.

'I prepared him in advance and told him that on Friday I would help him to feel safe to sleep in his own bed. When Friday evening came, we got ready for bed and read some stories. I told him that I was going to leave him to fall asleep by himself and then he started crying. I stayed with him, gently reassuring him that he would be safe and we would be in the next room. He cried for a while, and I stayed with him the whole time. When the crying slowed down I would gently let him know I was going to leave, and he started crying again. Eventually he fell asleep.

'The next day I noticed such a difference in him. He played for ages with his toys, whereas before he would be always asking to watch TV. He also played with his sisters without any arguments or aggression towards them. We listened for a few more nights and after that he was completely happy to sleep in his own bed. Sometimes he comes and sleeps with us again, and I don't mind because I know that the underlying fears aren't there anymore. I realised that helping him to sleep in his own bed was about so much more than just that. It was about noticing the places where he didn't feel good and helping him to feel better in his own skin.'

Both these case studies show how setting limits around sleep can help children to sleep better and also feel more closely connected to the parent that listens. The following example is about thumb-sucking, but a similar approach could also be used for using a dummy, or in other situations where a child relies on things being a certain way for sleep that mask their underlying feelings.

Case Study: Caroline

'My daughter has always been a thumb sucker, and from time to time I try to offer her play and connection to get her laughing when she retreats into sucking her thumb, particularly at bedtime.

'Occasionally, I'll set a limit, and hold her thumb and say, 'I'm sorry but I won't let you suck your thumb.' I see that she uses thumb-sucking as a coping mechanism for holding in feelings; for example, if she falls over she might cry for a few moments and then put her thumb in her mouth, or if we are in a group of people she might suck her thumb because she feels a bit shy.

'When she was a baby, I would notice that we felt much closer connected if I'd set a limit about thumb-sucking and staylistened to some feelings. I would also notice that when I did she wouldn't suck her thumb throughout the night but would sleep much longer and more deeply. The next day she'd be really joyful, smiling a lot and making lots of eye contact. It felt like there was something deep about the way we looked at each other – that I had made a really lasting connection with her by listening to her feelings.'

EXERCISE: **Reflection – think about your own sleep patterns**

1 What was sleep and bedtime like for you as a child? Tell your own history of how you have slept throughout your life.

2 Talk about the history of your child's sleeping patterns since they have been born. Be sure to talk about your own emotional reactions too.

EXERCISE: **Try this – bedtime special time**

1 Try ten minutes of special time in the evening, or ten minutes of rough-and-tumble/playlistening.

2 Notice if it makes bedtime feel more connected and go more smoothly.

3 Think about how you can add special time and/or rough-and-tumble/playlistening into your regular evening and bedtime routine.

CHAPTER 14

Separations and Long Goodbyes – Sending Your Child Off into the World

•

'Man's feelings are always purest and most
glowing in the hour of meeting and of farewell.'

Jean Paul Richter, author

Even as we build close connections with our children, separation is an inevitable part of life. It might be that we need
to send our child to day care or school, or we just want to have
a shower alone while another adult watches our baby. The time
that we spend apart from our baby and toddler is very individual
and depends on our circumstances.

Babies and children internalise a sense of their caregivers
as a safe base so that step by step they can go off and explore
the world. They need lots of time to bond and form strong
attachments with us before they do so. When they get older
it's up to us how much separation feels right for our family.
The most important thing is that our children feel happy and
connected when we say goodbye to them and that they are
being left with someone whom we trust and who loves and
supports them.

When children have multiple attachments to more than just

their parents, it expands their world and enriches their lives. It's actually a gift to help our child develop relationships with extended family or other caregivers. It's also essential that we get a break from time to time.

Using tools to ease separation anxiety

Separation anxiety is natural and common to all children, but we can use the Hand in Hand Parenting tools to help reduce it. Some children might find it relatively easy to separate from their parents, whereas others have a harder time. If our child was separated from us briefly after birth or for medical care, for example, this early hurt can be triggered at the moment of separation. Children also often experience a lot of separation anxiety when they have feelings to release and need our presence to help with them.

Crying is common at the moment when our babies or children need to separate from us, which can make us feel uncomfortable or guilty about leaving them. We might decide to rush away and be told later, by our partner or relative, or day care assistant, that our child stopped crying after we were gone and was fine. Or we might be encouraged to leave without saying goodbye at all, so that their feelings don't get triggered.

When we try to say goodbye, and our child objects, or cries or grabs our hand and wants to play with us, they are giving us an important message about how separation feels for them. If we rush away without listening to the feelings, this prevents our child healing from whatever makes it hard. If we rush away without saying goodbye at all, our child might feel completely confused. He might have increased anxiety, wondering if we might disappear without explanation at any moment, especially if he is very young.

With these scenarios our child might continue to cry every single time we leave. Or he might accept that he will never be listened to during separations and eventually stop crying about it. This can look as if he doesn't mind us going, when in actual fact he has just given up expressing how he feels. The feelings are still there and might come out at other times, or through off-track behaviour.

At the other extreme, we could assume that because our child cries when we try to leave, then he cannot handle being separated from us, even for a moment. So we might give up trying to be apart from him, even to go to the toilet alone. At first glance this looks like the kinder option, but we are actually avoiding his fears and anxieties rather than helping him with them.

The long goodbye

To help our child with feelings about separation, we need a partner or another caregiver that our child trusts and who understands the Hand in Hand Parenting approach. Instead of rushing off to try to avoid the feelings, we instead have a 'long goodbye', where we tell our child we need to leave, and then staylisten to whatever feelings arise. Being there while our child is upset helps to build their sense of connection so that they can feel more confident about saying goodbye.

When we leave, it's crucial that we explain to our child what's happening. Even while she is a baby, we should tell her where we are going and when we'll come back. We can never be sure when our child will begin to understand what we say, and she may also find our tone reassuring.

We can approach separations in the same way that we set limits. We gently explain that we need to go, and, if she starts to cry, we can hold her and listen fully to her upset. We can hug our child and reassure her that we will come back. If our child stops crying, then we can move towards giving her to her caregiver or, if she's older, putting her down and moving towards the door.

We can do this slowly and gradually, stopping if our child starts to cry, and staying with her. When she finishes crying we can try to go again.

When my daughter was about 15 months old she experienced a lot of separation anxiety in the evening, close to bedtime. If we were all in the room together and I needed to use the bathroom, she would start crying.

I sensed that this small separation was triggering larger fears about separation. It was her broken cookie. She loved and trusted her dad, and many times I would leave the room without her getting upset at all. By this age, I sensed she understood almost everything I said to her. I was pretty sure she understood when I told her I was just going to the bathroom and would be back in five minutes.

So I decided I would help her with the separation anxiety. I told her I needed to go and gradually moved towards the door. She came to me and started crying, and I kept holding her until she stopped, reassuring her that I would be back. If she stopped crying, I would move her a little bit closer to her dad's arms. She'd then start crying again. Gradually, I could move her into her dad's arms, waiting until she felt OK with it.

I then gradually moved out of the room, still talking to her and reassuring her that I would be back. If she cried, I would stop moving away and just stay where I was, or come a little closer and hold her again, so that she had a connection to me. Step by step I was able to get a little further out the door, while offering her lots of reassurance that she was safe and I would be back. After each wave of crying, the distance she felt safe to be away from me would lengthen.

After crying for a while, she suddenly flipped into laughter, crawling from one parent to the other, as I playfully tried to put her back with her dad. In the same way that laughter can turn to tears, tears can also turn into laughter.

Eventually I told her I was going to clean my teeth and she happily let me go, almost as if she had forgotten that she'd ever been upset about it. She was in a really happy mood, playing and laughing and enjoying the company of both her parents. After this she was back to her normal self, happy to be left with her dad if I needed to use the bathroom or pop out for a while. From time to time she'd get upset again and I would repeat the process, staying until she was happy for me to go.

The benefits of taking your time

Why listen about a small separation like this? I could have gone for the quick-fix option and just taken my daughter with me into the bathroom. But I knew that if I didn't listen to her, those clingy, anxious feelings would still be there under the surface, and that my daughter would pick another time to try to grab my attention about them. I wanted to listen when I had the time, rather than for the feelings to come up at another moment when I might have no choice but to separate quickly and not be able to listen to her upset.

Children choose small, everyday broken-cookie moments to work on their fear of separation. Listening when we have the time and the emotional resources means that when we do need to separate from our child the process is a lot less scary for them. Listening to our children's feelings about separation means that they can then happily and willingly let us go most of the time, provided they are left with an adult they like and trust. This means that we don't have to carry the guilt that we have left them crying or upset. When we work through our child's separation anxiety, we can see that they can tolerate being apart from us when they are loved and cared for well while we are away. They also feel safe and confident that we will return. Separation feels a lot better for everyone.

After working through her separation anxiety, my daughter was happy to be put to bed by my husband or by me. It was clear that I was still her primary attachment, but this didn't equate to me having to do everything for her. She didn't have a meltdown every single time I went to have a shower or her dad put her to bed, because she had let go of all those feelings. I'm sure that listening like this not only helped her confidence in separations but also gave her a strong bond with her dad.

When our children have worked through their feelings about separation, they can think clearly and respect our needs and wishes too. They can be in thinking mode about separation rather than feeling mode. I sometimes work at home writing, and I shut the door to my office while my daughter is looked after by her dad. She accepts that I'm busy and need time to work; however, if there is a time when she's low on connection she will definitely find a way to tell me about it!

We can use our child's feelings as an emotional compass, to notice just how much separation they can tolerate, and when they need more time with us to reconnect. Through giving them the connection they need, and listening when the feelings get hard, our goodbyes can always be happy ones.

Games to play to make separation easier

There may be times when your child isn't in the mood to cry about separation, but she is grabbing your hands or legs and not letting you go. Separation might also involve some laughter and play. With young babies, peek-a-boo is a game that helps children with separation and usually involves a lot of laughter. With older toddlers we could play a game called 'he's mine' where we involve a partner. We both try to hold on to our child, and gently pull him from one parent to the other, saying 'he's mine'. Our child gets a double dose of love and connection.

We could also try some power reversal, and tell our toddler, 'I hope you don't push me out of the door' in a way that invites them to play. We could let them push us out and then come back in and exclaim, 'Hey! I'm not ready to go, I need some more kisses.'

One day, while writing this book, my daughter, my husband and I took the train into town together. I was going off to work in the library while they were going to do some shopping. When we got off the train, my daughter started pulling me in the direction of the shops. She was obviously not happy to be separated from me. Luckily, I was able to think quickly enough to turn it into a game. I would let her pull me, and would fling myself forward and then pull her ahead of me, and she would start laughing as we ran along together. Then I would exclaim, 'Oh no, this isn't the way I meant to go!' and start walking the other way, pulling her back with me. Then I'd let her pull me back towards the shops again.

We repeated this a few times, until we got to the escalators that went to the shops. Then my daughter said, 'You can go now, I just wanted to pull you to the escalators', and off I went. Instead of going away with guilt, I had the warm sense that I'd met her need for connection and she was happy for me to go. When she was free of her feelings she could understand and respect my need to work.

Reinforcing your child's security

Through listening to feelings about separation, children internalise a sense of their parent as a secure base so that they can go off and explore the world. They can have a richer life, feeling safe to explore, whether it's a baby crawling to the other side of the room or a toddler going to a dance class.

Small separations can feel like a big deal to our children. If we have the time and energy to play or to listen to upsets it's always an investment. It builds our child's trust that we are always there when they need us. They understand we care about their feelings and will help them. As they grow older they'll know they can come to us when life gets hard.

Leaving when the time is right can actually build the connection with your child, because you notice all the little moments in which your child has separation fears that get in the way of internalising their close connection with you. In this way, separating from our children can actually bring us closer together.

On returning

While our children are away from us, their feelings might get triggered: they might miss us; they might be getting to know and trust a new caregiver; or they might experience difficult or challenging experiences that they find hard to navigate without us. It doesn't necessarily mean that separation from our children is a completely negative experience, but it does mean that even if our children willingly separate from us they might tell us about their feelings when they return.

One morning when my daughter was two, my friend babysat her while I went to a day-long meeting. When I dropped my daughter off she was happy and really excited, and ready to spend the day with my friend and her daughter, who is my daughter's best friend. She pushed me away and told me to go. It seemed like she was excited to be going off on her big adventure, although I sensed that behind that playful push was a bit of fear and anxiety at being away from me.

My husband picked her up and I got a message from my friend to say that they'd had a great time. When I returned home my daughter immediately asked to play with my mobile phone. The fact that she asked me for it the minute I walked through the door made me sense that what she really needed was connection with me, so I said no.

She cried for a few moments, saying, 'I want mummy's phone', and then suddenly changed to 'I want mummy', and she came to hug me. It was clear that I'd guessed right about the real reason behind her apparent need for my phone. I knew my daughter had enjoyed her day, but feelings to the contrary had also been triggered. It was the longest she'd been with anyone other than me, apart from her dad.

When we return to our children they might bring us stories, encoded in their emotions and behaviour, of how the separation was for them. Perhaps she fell over, or perhaps another child at pre-school ran into her and she got a fright. Perhaps she is simply getting used to being away from us for a longer stretch of time.

She might cry at the time, or she might store up her feelings until she is back with us, the people children feel most safe to be upset with. As long as we keep listening, our children will always bring us these stories. In this way, even though we separate from them, we can always be fully part of their lives.

Listening time to help untangle our feelings about separation

Our children aren't the only ones that have strong emotions about separating. Leaving our babies or toddlers can be nerve-wracking for us parents too. We sometimes have our own separation anxiety to deal with.

When our children have trouble separating from us it's essential that we have some listening time. Children can pick up on our feelings, so if we feel anxious about leaving them, this makes separation harder for them.

If, at any time, a particular separation doesn't feel good, listening time can help us to work out why. Perhaps deep down we don't feel confident about the quality of care our child is receiving, or we have our own past hurts about separation. Listening time can help us untangle our own instincts about how we feel about the separation from our own history.

Sometimes, if we had disconnected relationships with our parents, we can overcompensate, feeling that if we risk spending any time away from our children we will break the connection with them. Or we might do the opposite and find it hard to be with our children for longer periods. We need time to talk about our own childhood so that these feelings aren't clouding our thinking. Then it becomes easier to make a good judgement and work out which kinds of separations are good for everyone in the family.

During listening time you can talk about any confusion or sadness you feel. You can make your feelings as big as you like, without fear of someone telling you not to worry and that it will be fine. Often a simple separation can trigger all the bigger fears and anxieties we have about our children. Will they be safe when they are out in the world? Will they still love us when they are teenagers? Giving our fears a voice will allow us to become confident parents, who feel calm and patient enough to be there to listen to our children about separation. We will no longer be clouded by our own feelings.

Ultimately, as we listen to ourselves and to our children we both feel better about separation. Our children can internalise the sense of feeling safe and connected to us so that when they grow and fly the nest, they will still feel us with them. I love this idea that when we connect and interact with our children we are interweaving ourselves together so that we will never really be apart.

Case Study: Melanie

'My son had severe separation anxiety, which I think was because I went away for a couple of weeks for work when he was just a young baby. When he was four, he still didn't feel comfortable staying with anyone apart from me or his father.

'I decided to start an emotional project, and began to play lots of playlistening games around separation. I would hold him tight and tell him I was never going to let him go, and then let him escape. Then I'd act all upset in a playful way, saying, "Oh whoops! He left me. What am I going to do now?"

'Then we played a game with a long measuring tape, and I'd say, "Let's see how far apart we can be from each other", and I'd measure the distance. Then he would run and start laughing, saying, "See how far I can be away from you", and I would say, "No, no, no, that's too far!", mirroring his own separation anxiety.

'I talked to a friend of mine who knows all about listening to crying, and I told my son that he would spend the day with her in a few weeks time. He started to cry, and I listened. I prepared him in advance, and every day or so I'd bring the subject up again, and he would start crying about it. He cried for a long time when I had to leave him at my friend's.

'Later, when I went to pick him up, I could see that he was more relaxed, talking happily about all the things they had done together.

'I started to go out with my husband more. One time we went out for dinner, and when I told my son he started crying, asking all these anxious questions about where I was going and how long I'd be. By the evening of the dinner he was absolutely fine, and happy to be left with a babysitter he knew well.

'He started kindergarten when he was five, and cried a lot at the moment of separation, even though he was happy at the kindergarten and liked what they did there. It took about six months before he could happily go there without me. I think it took a long time because of those long, early separations, but it was worth it, as he loves going to kindergarten now. I also feel so much better having worked through the separation anxiety, knowing that it's OK that I didn't know everything perfectly from that start but that I could help him heal later.'

EXERCISE: Reflection – remember your own separations

1   How do you feel about possible separations from your child? What are your biggest fears and anxieties, hopes and dreams for your child?

2   Can you remember what it was like when you separated from your parents to go to a playgroup, day care, nursery or school?

EXERCISE: Try this – a long goodbye

Next time you need to separate from your baby or toddler, and he gets upset, try a long goodbye – even if it's just to pop to the toilet or the shower. Listen to his feelings so that when you need to separate for real and don't have so much time to listen, he will be less likely to get upset because he has already released some of his separation anxiety.

CHAPTER 15

Public Meltdowns – Staying
Cool Out in the World

•

'To free us from the expectations of others, to
give us back to ourselves – there lies the great,
singular power of self-respect.'

Joan Didion, author

Emotional expression is essential for our child's well-being,
but what about crying and tantrums in public, or when we
are with friends and family? We can feel like everyone's eyes and
judgements are upon us. We can often receive unsolicited advice
about what our child needs or what we should do to stop the
crying. We don't want to disturb others, so how do we balance
their needs with the needs of our children?

Our children sense when it is a good time to release feelings.
They would actually much rather cry in private where they feel
our full attention on us. When we learn and practise the Hand
in Hand Parenting tools, our children will have most of their
meltdowns at home when they sense we are more available to
listen. Listening to tears, rather than distracting and stopping
them, also means that children can release more of their feelings so that there's much less chance that they will spill out in
public.

Babies and toddlers generally show more of their feelings at home. Sometimes, parents mistake this grouchiness for a child being bored and needing more stimulation, so they spend more time out of the house. Often, it's not because home is boring but just because there's less going on; our child senses that there's more chance of having our full attention, so they begin to 'act up' or express some feelings.

Using the strategies to avoid public meltdowns

We can prevent many public meltdowns simply by using the Hand in Hand Parenting tools as much as possible. We can do regular special time, notice when our child is off-track and set limits, as well as spending plenty of time playing, laughing and staylistening, if necessary. This means that when we do go out they will be feeling well connected. Even so, it's inevitable that there will be times when public meltdowns happen.

Listening to tears in public is not easy. The adults around us might react strongly. Their own unconscious memories of how they were treated when they cried as children can be triggered. They might respond with advice that is intended to be helpful or with judgemental looks. In these moments our limbic system senses both the emotional upset of our child as well as that of the adults around us. It's no wonder we feel stressed! There is such a strong underlying message in our society that tears are not allowed, or that stopping tears equates with cheering a child up, that many people feel compelled to intervene.

One morning, I was on the train with my daughter who was going off to her playgroup. She was crying because she wanted to eat chocolate. I was pretty sure that the crying about chocolate was triggered because she was feeling nervous about separating from me but was unable to put these feelings into words. I wanted to listen to her so that she could feel genuinely confident about leaving me rather than just dampening down the feeling with chocolate. Just then the lady sitting opposite me reached into her bag and offered me some chocolate for my daughter! It almost seems like there are people everywhere with sweets and presents ready for the crying children they might meet! These kinds of situations can be frustrating when we want to take time to listen to our children. It also shows just how hard adults find it to listen to tears.

How to listen in public

When upsets happen in public, the best thing to do is to listen whenever possible, as we would normally do. Obviously, there will be occasions when listening is impossible, such as a wedding ceremony, for example. In this case, we can use some distraction tactics.

It's a good idea to find some privacy, so that other people aren't feeling disturbed and we can listen to our child without being interrupted. If privacy is not possible, we can still listen as best we can. It's actually a good example for other parents to see us modelling empathetic listening and staying calm, rather than ignoring or shouting at our child. They can see what stay-listening with warmth really looks like, and how effective it can be. They may also become more relaxed themselves because they see how well you are handling it.

One time, when my daughter was about two years old, I went to have lunch with a friend. My daughter was tense and finding it hard to relax in a new environment with my friend whom she didn't know very well. She ate some yoghurt, and then wanted to get down from the table, but I wanted to clean her face first. When I told her I needed to clean her face, she started to cry.

My friend was there all ready to swoop in with a tissue as she was crying. I asked her if she would just wait a second. I held my daughter until she stopped crying, then I cleaned her face without an objection. My friend said, 'I like what you did there. Was that something you learnt on your parenting course?'

Here was a great demonstration of setting limits and staylistening in action: a way of not forcing my child to do something against her will but waiting until she felt OK with it. After that we happily played on my friend's indoor trampoline together. My daughter was feeling much more relaxed and comfortable in my friend's company.

When we staylisten in public we are delivering a powerful message to the world: that we are OK with crying. Perhaps other parents will be inspired and ask what our secret is.

Finding the time and patience when out of the house

Listening in public works as long as we have the patience to listen. We may notice that our children don't cry for as long, or we don't listen so connectedly, because we're both conscious of the outside world. When we respond automatically to our children's upsets, a lot of that is rooted in wondering what the people around us think about the crying. We feel we must stop the crying.

When I was a new mother trying to work out what was this thing about crying, I felt nervous and edgy whenever my daughter got upset in public. As I reached out to the other parents who were parenting in similar ways and built a community around me of friends and listening partners, my confidence grew.

Once we were on a train going out for dinner. My daughter was having a tantrum because she was frustrated and couldn't put the lid back on a water bottle. After just a few seconds of crying a couple moved seats and the woman walked off with her fingers in her ears. I didn't want to purposely disturb anyone, but I knew that if I helped my daughter with her feelings, she would be much more relaxed and at ease for the rest of the journey. She only cried for a few minutes. Despite the negative reaction, I felt wrapped up in a warm bubble listening to my daughter's feelings, regardless of how I was being judged. My first priority was taking care of my daughter and helping her feel better.

Later, at the restaurant, my daughter was happy and content. It would have disturbed everyone if she continued to be moany and whiny for the rest of the evening.

This experience made me realise just how powerful it is to feel confident in our own conviction, and to have a supportive community of people who also understand the healing power of tears. That day on the train my listening partners felt like invisible angels on my shoulders, so that I felt safe knowing there were others who supported me even if I was out in public on my own.

Slowing life down to listen

We have busy lives, and sometimes tantrums in public can be an indication that we need to slow down a bit. Children might get stressed and overwhelmed, or just need some downtime to play and hang out with us at home and release a backlog of emotions.

When my daughter was adjusting to a new playgroup, she really liked to be at home for the rest of the day and even told me, 'I can only do one thing per day!' Some days I'd try to pack things in and over-scheduled us a bit.

One afternoon I arranged to meet a friend in town after my daughter's playgroup, and my daughter was very moany and whiny and seemed on the verge of a tantrum. We went to the toilet and she started crying because I had gone to the toilet first. I could hear a woman in the other toilet muttering about the noise. I was late to meet my friend.

Listening in public helps our children, but we are not as fully relaxed as we might be at home. We have places to go and people to see, and we may not always be fully focused on our child. It's sometimes hard to relax when we are conscious of other people's reactions. If our children are having frequent public meltdowns, or lots of off-track behaviour, it might be a sign that they need some time at home to relax and decompress. In this way our

children reach emotional equilibrium and can also be our teachers, guiding us towards more balance in our lives.

Towards a world of listening

Every time we listen to our child in public we are helping to
create a different environment, one in which children's emotions are fully accepted. As well as setting our own example, we
can be supportive of other parents out there in the world. When
we get listened to ourselves, we have an adult who empathises
with us, no matter what our struggles are, and no matter how
many parenting mistakes we've made.

As we are listened to ourselves, we might automatically start
extending that empathy to other parents around us. If we see a
parent getting angry or a child crying, we might find that instead
of judging them or getting irritated by the noise, we see that both
parent and child are having a hard time.

If we notice other parents struggling, we can give them a
supportive smile. They might be getting angry or about to lose
patience. They may be feeling the pressure of trying to keep
their child quiet in public as society often expects. A smile, a
few words, or just an empathetic look if it comes naturally, can
help them feel understood and accepted. Even the fact that we're
present in the world, not being so reactive towards their child's
emotional outbursts, can take the pressure off. By being listened
to ourselves, and healing our own feelings, we'll notice that
we have more understanding and acceptance of other people's
emotions. We can be that non-judgemental parent who knows
it gets tough sometimes.

Case Study: Elizabeth

'When my daughter was four we went to a toy shop to
buy a present for her friend. My daughter asked if we
could buy a baby doll. She had been whiny for a while,

and I sensed that she needed to cry. I said no, telling her we already had lots of dolls at home.

'She grabbed the doll and ran outside the shop. I followed after her, quickly telling the shop assistant that I would return the doll, but I wouldn't take it off her straight away, because she seemed quite upset.

'I caught up with her, and touched the doll and her hand. I told her that we needed to return it. She started crying. I knelt down next to her and listened. From time to time, I'd remind her that we needed to take it back, but I kept my hand on her hand, rather than grabbing the doll away immediately. She cried for a while, and then she suddenly stopped and said, "OK. I'll put the doll back, but please can I have it for Christmas?" I said "perhaps".

'As I listened, a lot of people were walking by, but because I've had a lot of experience with crying in public I didn't feel too embarrassed. I've seen the results afterwards. I knew that she'd be more cooperative and relaxed, so it was worth it. I was also afraid I would miss my chance if I didn't listen there and then. I was feeling calm and had the patience to listen, and I don't always feel that way.'

I love the following story, which shows how we can turn things around for other parents when we move away from judging them to supporting them instead.

Case Study: Zoe – a Hand in Hand Parenting instructor

'I'm feeling really proud of how an interaction went in the supermarket yesterday. There was a mum pushing a trolley around, she had two-year-old twins in the seats at the front and another boy of about three or four years old with her. I had seen her and thought what a sweet little family it was.

'After a few minutes in the shop I could hear the boy was having a major meltdown in an aisle close by. This was going on for quite a few minutes and he was screaming so that the whole store could hear him. I felt quite emotional hearing him cry and wondered whether I would dare to approach the mum and offer support. I was nervous about doing this, not knowing how she would react in such a stressful situation, but resolved to brave it and see if I could support her in some way.

'I manoeuvred my trolley so that I was approaching her from the front and not behind. She was crouched on the floor holding the child who was still screaming. I gently approached and made eye contact and said, "You're doing a great job here." She looked at me, eyes full of tears and said, "I feel like crying." I placed my hand on her back and again, with lots of eye contact, reassured her that I had been right where she was now and asked if there was anything I could do to help. She started explaining to me about her parenting approach, that she would normally use time out, but she couldn't do that in the shop, and that she wouldn't spank the child in this situation, only if he was to run in the road or something like that. I listened to her with my full attention, keeping my hand on her back, and again reassured her that she was doing a great job. She then asked me to go and get her some raisins as that was the last item she needed and then she could leave the shop. I went and did that for her. When I got back two minutes later, the child had stopped crying, mum was hugging him and all seemed much calmer. She thanked me for coming over and I walked off feeling like my heart would burst from happiness that I had been able to support this family in this little way and that it worked out so well.'

EXERCISE: Reflection – thinking about public meltdowns

1   Can you remember some moments when your baby or tod-
    dler was crying in public or around friends or family? How
    did you feel and how did you react?

2   Notice the feelings that come up in you when another child
    cries in public. What sort of feelings get stirred in you?
    What sorts of judgements do you have about the child or
    the parent? Let it out in a listening time and see if that gives
    you a different perspective on the situation.

3   What would have happened if you had cried in public as
    a child?

EXERCISE: Try this – slow down

Do some special time before leaving the house. Next time your
child has a meltdown in public, try to slow down and tune into
your child's needs. Can you find a quiet space to listen to her?

CHAPTER 16

A Little Special Time for Your Partner – Keeping the Parental Relationship Strong

•

'Someone to tell it to is one of the fundamental needs of human beings.'

Miles Franklin, writer

Parenting can enrich the relationship we have with our partner. As we work together to care for a new living being, we grow and develop in our partnership too. It can be one of the most rewarding experiences of our lives; however, the challenges of parenting can cause rocky moments in even the most stable of relationships. We invest so much time and energy in our children that we can sometimes neglect the foundation upon which our family life was built: the relationship with our partner.

As well as nurturing our children and ourselves, let's not forget the other important relationship in our lives. When we are happy in our partnership we can share this happiness with our children.

You might be reading this wondering how to reignite the spark in your relationship or how to have important conversations with your partner about what you've read in this book and how you want to parent.

If you are together with the co-parent of your children, I hope this chapter will help inspire you to keep that relationship strong. If you are a single parent, I hope it will still have some value, with suggestions on how to broach important topics with your ex-partner, and how to work together to parent your children.

Luckily, the Hand in Hand Parenting tools work on adults too. We can use the art of listening to improve communication with our partner and grab little moments of laughter and one-to-one time with each other. We can keep our sense of connection strong, even when life is busy. We can remember the relationship we had before children and recover it after challenging times.

Before my daughter was born, I always vowed that I would not let having a baby change my relationship with my husband. We were very happily married and felt like soul mates; however, I had no idea just how all-encompassing having a baby was.

After my daughter was born, all my energy went towards looking after her, and whenever she was sleeping I would read parenting books, trying to work out how to be a good mother. I missed my husband, who seemed like a distant figure in my life. I would often be snappy with him. All my efforts went towards being a patient mum, and I didn't have much patience left for my husband.

Things only started to change when I suddenly realised that being a 'good' parent wasn't just about caring for my daughter. It also meant nurturing the relationship with my husband. If I could try to be patient with him, to find moments to listen to him or give him attention, this would, by extension, mean he would have more patience and attention for our daughter. Not only that but we'd both feel happier and more connected too. My daughter would absorb our happiness.

Families operate as a whole. If we are all happy, loved and nurtured, family life goes much more smoothly. We can also be a good model for our children to see how we interact and communicate with our partner.

Finding time for each other in a busy life

It's natural that in our busy lives we may be rushing around meeting our child's needs and not giving much thought to what our partner needs. After all, our children are helpless and completely dependent on us, whereas our partner is an adult. When life gets busy, our connection with our partner is often the first thing we let slip. I once saw a couple on the tram passionately kissing while their five-year-old son was being ignored on the seat beside them, but I'm sure this is the exception rather than the rule in most families! A lot of the time our children will barely let us have a conversation together and will jump in between any kiss or hug. Their need for connection is so strong.

When we practise the tools, we may notice that our children's sense of connection becomes stronger, and there will be moments here and there where we can connect with our partner and even have a bit of a conversation. But often we need to wait until we are alone with our partner before we can interact properly.

We might find that most of our interactions with our partner are when we're on the go, clearing up the kitchen or getting dinner ready, and that we rarely spend time just sitting down together, hanging out. A little can go a long way when it comes to our partner. Sometimes, just attuning to them and setting an intention to give them more attention can be really helpful. If we are talking to them while multi-tasking, perhaps we can just slow down for a moment so that we can really look at them or listen. We can remember to give them a hug, and appreciate them for what they do. We can remember to have little moments of connection sprinkled throughout the day in the same way that we do with our children. We can ask our partner how their day was and take time to listen to the answer.

Giving our partner a dose of our undivided attention can be powerful. Perhaps we can remind ourselves to notice what makes them laugh, and find moments here and there where we slow down and be playful or laugh with each other.

Practising special time with your partner

When my daughter was a year old my mum came to stay with us for a week. On the Sunday afternoon my husband and I nipped out for a 15-minute bike ride together. For those 15 minutes it was like going back in time to before we had a baby. I felt so free cycling on my bike, chatting and laughing with him. I was surprised to find that during the days after our bike ride I felt closer to him.

Later, I realised that the bike ride had been our form of special time. That spending concentrated quality time is something we can do with our partners as well as our children. It wasn't necessary to have a big chunk of time. Fifteen minutes could bring us closer together. Just like our children, we internalise the sense of togetherness, so it is still there after the special time is finished.

When we think of rebuilding closeness with a partner after having a baby, we tend to focus on the obvious sex part, or on having a date night; however, in the early stages of parenting we might not have the time or energy. Luckily, just five minutes can make a difference. We can make a point of telling our partner about special time, and setting a timer, taking it in turns to choose something to do. It could be as simple as just sitting on the sofa chatting for five minutes, or listening to a favourite song together.

We can also do something called 'unannounced special time', where we just make an intention with ourselves to hang out with our partner for a set length of time, and give them some warm attention. If we think our partner might find the idea of special time a bit cheesy, this is the perfect compromise.

What would help you to remember to connect with your partner? Perhaps you could draw a love heart on a Post-it note and put it on the fridge door, or put a wooden love heart in your pocket to remind yourself to focus on your relationship. Scheduling time doesn't seem like a romantic idea, but in the busy early days of parenting it might be essential to fix a special-time date on the calendar just to make sure that it happens.

Sharing parenting understanding

As you work through this book, you may be wondering how to share with your partner the wonderful information that you have learnt. I think that one of the best building blocks for beginning to share this information is to connect with our partner. Just like connection breeds cooperation with our children, it can help with our partner too. When we attune to our partner, and spend time talking, laughing and enjoying each other's company, we will communicate and understand each other better, and be more likely to find compromise and common ground.

You could explain to your partner a little about this book, and suggest that they read it too. You could also share articles from the Hand in Hand Parenting website, or take an online course and watch the videos together. That can be a nice way to do it, because learning can then become a time of connection with each other.

Many people are resistant to the idea of learning about parenting. Your co-parent might think it's a bit unnatural to take a course where someone tells you how to parent. They might assume, rightly so, that they are the best expert on their kids and that they can follow their instincts. They may not understand that the Hand in Hand Parenting approach is one that can help us attend more closely to our parenting instincts to listen and connect, and be calm and patient without our emotional baggage getting in the way.

It might be a slow process for your partner to get on board.

When parents see children displaying emotions but who are not punished or given consequences, they may have their own strong reactions to their emotions, particularly if they had a difficult childhood themselves and haven't reflected on it much. They might automatically think that the way they were parented is a good model.

Time will prove the benefits

As your family evolves for the better, your partner will start to see that what you are doing works. You are a great model. Having these tools will give you solutions for almost any parenting situation you find yourself in. You partner will see you handle upsets and off-track behaviour with confidence and ease.

You could give them a few tips, as long as this can be done in a sensitive, thoughtful way. You might want to explain a bit about crying, saying something like, 'I've noticed that if I just give them a hug, without trying to distract or fix the situation, they can get their emotions out and feel much better.'

As your partner observes you parenting, by listening to your children's emotions and making them laugh, it may be that parenting conversations naturally begin, and you can start to articulate what you have learnt. When your partner sees you listening to your children's emotional upsets, they might become angry. He or she might feel that you are simply encouraging your child to act up. Sometimes it just takes observing your child coming out of the other side of their emotions for your partner to see how effective it is to just listen. Perhaps they'll notice your child being less off-track and realise that this approach really works.

Your partner's resistance to listening to emotions might stem from the fact that they weren't parented in this way, and it brings up many hurt feelings from the past. Rational explanations of how the tools work may not be effective in the moment if your partner feels angry or irritated by your child's emotional outbursts or behaviour.

Forcing and pressurising your partner to read about Hand in Hand Parenting, or to parent in a certain way, won't help if he or she is feeling emotional. That's one of the reasons why it's so important that we give our partner attention and connection whenever we can. In little ways we can help our partner with the emotions that get in the way of being unconditionally supportive of their children.

We are all on a particular path when it comes to healing and parenting. Hand in Hand Parenting involves deep emotional healing work, and it's not something that everyone is interested in doing. Some will just dip their toes in; others will dive in.

My husband listens to my daughter's feelings, and plays and laughs with her, but he is just not interested in having a listening partnership, even though he's heard me go on and on about the benefits enough times to understand that it works!

Staylistening between partners

You and your partner are both adults. You are able to control your emotions much better than your children do, but your emotional lives are just as complex. We actually need emotional connection just as much as our children do, and things are made doubly complicated because we didn't always have a deep sense of connection when we were children.

We will have conflicts and difficulties with our partners, and when we get stressed our own past hurts rise to the surface. This makes it hard to think and work out what to do in the present.

If my husband comes home from work and is quiet and a bit moody because he's had a hard day, this doesn't combine well with my stress at the end of the day and my need to have someone to talk to. When I get stressed, I am reminded about my own past hurts, the times I felt alone or ignored as a child. I then project that on to my husband and start to feel paranoid and alone, sensing an uneasy vibe in the air. This situation could turn into an argument, if I complain that he's not listening to me, for example, or if he gets irritated that I'm not giving him space. In reality, we both just need to decompress.

Other common examples might be when a partner gets angry because they are worried about money, or when one parent feels the other is not strict enough with parenting or is feeding the children too much junk food. Often these worries and anxieties relate to the parent's own childhood stories, although it's not always easy to remember that in the heat of the moment.

What we learn about listening to children, and to other adults during our listening time, doesn't always automatically extend into other aspects of our lives. We tend to go back on to autopilot, offering advice when our partner is upset, or getting impatient if they start ranting.

We can't turn everyday conversation into a listening time, but we can employ some of the principles to help our communication and connection. When your partner is angry or upset, you may get too emotional to be able to listen from a neutral standpoint. You might be being blamed for the upset, or even if the upset is unrelated to you, you might just lack the patience to listen.

It's good to remind ourselves that our partner might not mean what they say. If they are feeling over-emotional, their pre-frontal cortex won't be functioning well. They probably aren't thinking through what they are saying and may just need to express themselves.

When we staylisten with a baby or toddler, it doesn't usually involve a lot of words. When adults vent, on the other hand, they will tend to talk a lot. We can then get into the trap of trying to converse and talk, to offer solutions or to try to fix the situation.

We can employ some of the principles of staylistening when our partner is angry or upset. We can listen without trying to fix or offer solutions. As long as we've got the emotional energy to listen, we can let them vent. When we stay calm, the other person can let their emotions go. Afterwards, they might even attune to our sense of calm and peace, and feel better themselves.

If your partner is directing anger at you, listening may not be possible. It's a good idea to set limits on language or things that your partner says to you that are hurtful and unfair.

These principles help, but we shouldn't be expected to be the sole listener in our partner's life, especially if the listening is not reciprocated. If they are struggling, they might need a listening partner of their own.

Remembering to listen to each other

My husband has always been a pretty good listener, but like many of us, he tends to incline towards fixing or offering solutions. After learning about Hand in Hand Parenting I started noticing that I really wanted him to listen to me instead of giving advice. I was beginning to undo the pattern of trying to fix and stop feelings, and it started to feel very abrupt to have the process interrupted by his solutions, although because I loved and trusted him deeply it was very easy to cry with him.

Although he's never taken a formal class in Hand in Hand Parenting, I have told him about the listening process. Sometimes, when he tried to solve my problems, I would tell him, 'I think I just need to cry.' Now he tries to fix things slightly less frequently. He's never going to replace my listening partners, but it feels important that we can talk about the things that matter in our lives.

Some partners fully embrace the Hand in Hand Parenting approach, take a course themselves, and learn how to listen to adults as well as children; however, not everyone likes the idea of opening up their feelings, even if we think it would be good for them.

Our partners may never give us the kind of listening that we are used to from our listening partners, and we shouldn't expect it. If we find we are relying on them to be our sole listener, it's

probably a good idea to find another listening partner or schedule some listening time with someone else.

That doesn't mean we don't talk with our spouse about what's
going on in our lives or express our feelings. Communication
helps us to stay close. It just helps that we have an outlet, where
we can say whatever we want with someone who won't get tangled up in the emotional intricacies of our lives.

Using listening time to release thoughts about our relationship

Listening time can help us to process our thoughts about our
partnership and our parenting. We can set aside some of our
listening time to talk about how our relationship is going. We
can talk about what's going well, what's not going so well, and
work out how we want things to be.

If you are feeling angry, disappointed or frustrated with your
partner, one powerful technique is to express all that to your
listening partner instead. You can talk about the grief you may
feel that you are not as close to your partner anymore. This helps
when we need to have important discussions with our spouse.
We can go back with a clearer head, and not feel so emotionally
charged.

It's often worth using listening time to reflect on our own
parents' relationship. There may be some ways in which we
are unconsciously repeating our parents' struggles. We can talk
about any earlier times in our lives that our current struggles
remind us of. Listening time can help us break this cycle so that
we can create the relationship we want with our partner.

When counselling is appropriate

When it comes to having a happy family, nurturing ourselves
and our relationships is so important. There are, however, times

when one or both parents are deeply unhappy in a relationship and they don't know how to fix it. They might need some professional couples' counselling to help think about what to do. Although this chapter focuses on partners staying together and working things through, just like any other aspect of our lives, we need to nurture our own desires and needs, because this is essential for the happiness of our children.

Parenting can transform our relationship, and Hand in Hand Parenting can help us deepen our connection to our partner. Just like our children, our partners can be like a key to find the places where we are hurt so that we can heal and return to joyful presence with each other. Life gets busy, and there are many challenges along the way for our relationship, but we can return again and again to the love we have for each other.

Case Study: Emily

'My husband didn't like the Hand in Hand Parenting approach at first, especially special time and staylistening. He felt that special time created too many arguments in our house, because we have three children who would always fight about who went first, and who went second, and who had special time with mummy and who with daddy.

'Then, after two or three months, our children got used to having special time. It seemed like their cups were fuller because I was using the Hand in Hand Parenting tools and listening to their feelings on a regular basis. My husband began to see how they were learning negotiation skills by talking about who would have special time first and who would have it next. They also waited for their turn without complaint because they knew it would come eventually and that I always did my best to make things fair.

'My husband also had trouble with the staylistening, as he saw how angry the children would get sometimes and how they would hit or kick. He saw these strong expressions of emotion as disobedience. Then he began to see it working – how relaxed and calm they were afterwards. He started supporting me by staying with the other children if I was listening to one of them.

'He also tried to listen himself, although he's not great at it. He still talks a lot to work out what's going on and fix the situation, or to try to distract them. I sense he's not completely comfortable with their upsets.

'Nowadays, I try to let him do more of the listening, rather than just rushing in and taking over. I also give him a few tips, which I try to do in a gentle way, saying something like, "Hmmm, you could do it like this." I try to make sure I don't sound abrupt or critical.

'He's definitely changing; he shouts less these days, and he's come to respect my opinion about parenting much more.'

EXERCISE: Reflection – looking at your relationship with your partner

1 What did you and your partner love to do before your child was born? Is there a way that you can find time to do it?

2 What was your parents' relationship like? Can you remember a time when they fought? Were they affectionate to each other, and did they seem happy? Talk about whatever memories this question brings to mind.

3 Go through each of the tools and see how they might work with your partner: special time, taking turns, choosing something you love to do.

▶

4 How is your relationship with your partner going? What's going well? What's not going so well?

5 How would you like your relationship to be? Is it possible?

EXERCISE: Try this – adult special time

Try special time with your partner. Take it in turns to choose something that you'd like to do.

CHAPTER 17

Healing Broken Connections – Why it's Never Too Late to Recover and Repair

•

'There is an ancient tribal proverb I once heard in
India. It says that before we can see properly we
must first shed our tears to clear the way.'

Libba Bray

Throughout life, many events happen that can cause stress and disconnection in our families. A lot of these events are completely out of our control. Grief, divorce, accidents, or even positive changes like moving house or visiting relatives can fracture the sense of close connection we long for with our children.

When life is stressful, or we're going through emotional difficulties ourselves, it can be hard to listen to our children's feelings and deal with their off-track behaviour. What makes things even more challenging is that our children's behaviour can get harder to handle, just when our patience is running low.

It might be that this period of broken connection is a brief one, or that it goes back further. We might feel a sense of disconnection with our child because of the way their life started off. If we had a stressful pregnancy or birth, if we had post-natal depression or a difficult start to parenting, this can make it hard to bond with our child. Or if we didn't know about how to listen to feelings from the very beginning, we might find that parenting has been really challenging. Whatever the reason, we can take steps to begin to heal a broken connection and catch up on the times when we weren't able to listen or didn't know how.

As mentioned earlier, when my daughter was two years old, my grandmother died. I was devastated. I wasn't able to play with her as much, or give her the quality attention that she was used to. She began expressing to me how she was feeling with lots of difficult behaviour, such as hitting me, pretending to be a baby and suffering from separation anxiety. Because I was upset myself it was hard to be the calm listener she needed to release her own upsets.

I am not sure if it is just looking back through rose-tinted glasses, but I remember that before my grandmother's death my daughter was mostly happy or only sometimes crying. Either way, her emotions were always flowing freely. Now there seemed to be many more in-between times when she was whiny or grumpy, and her feelings were stuck. I was feeling pretty stuck too. It was disheartening dealing with the heavy grief as well as more challenging behaviour from my daughter. I couldn't be playful with her and try to get her laughing, or do much special time. I was in survival mode, just doing the basic tasks that were necessary to get through the day. It took time and lots of listening time for me to heal enough to be able to feel strong enough to help her properly with her feelings.

At first, the situation might seem overwhelming. We have our own strong emotions to deal with and also our child's. It can feel like a vicious cycle when we try to reconnect with our child while we are in a depleted state and we are met with an onslaught of challenging behaviour. If the disconnection has been there since the very beginning, we might feel like our child has a difficult or challenging personality.

We all do our best as parents to minimise our children's upsets and difficulties, but sometimes things happen that are difficult for us to control – or they are completely out of our control. Whatever has happened, it's always possible to rebuild the connection between you and your child. Discovering the healing power of tears means that we can help our children to make sense of what's happened and leave the past behind. We can begin a new relationship with our child just by beginning to listen to them.

Your listening time is your lifeline

The first step is to get more listening time for yourself. We need to release the feelings that have built up from dealing with the difficulties in our lives. We could ask our current listening partners if they'd be interested in exchanging more time, or perhaps look for a few more listening partners.

It's so essential that we take this first step of nurturing ourselves, even if we feel as if we don't need to and can manage alone. Often, the reason we get stuck in big struggles is that we are used to managing our emotions without enough support. We were trained to manage our emotions alone as children and have a tendency to continue to do so as adults. We might not ask for the support we really need because we have never experienced it and didn't grow up to expect it. We might need to be proactive to build the community we need because other parents are in the same position and also struggle to reach out.

We can use our current listening time to work out the logistics of who we might ask to be a listening partner or what other steps we need to take. Sometimes, just talking about how difficult it is to find the time for listening time, or to find parents whose schedule matches ours, can clear our head so that we can work out a way to make it work.

When I was writing this book, I needed a lot of listening time to work through some of the fears and anxieties that were provoked in me about the creative process. After crying about feeling unsupported and that I felt that no one wanted to help me, I then realised that I did have a couple of listening partners that I hadn't been in contact with for a while. I got in contact and they were happy to hear from me. The feeling of being unsupported was not due to my present situation; I did have people I could reach out to, but past hurts from times when I felt alone made it hard for me to reach out to someone.

This extra support is essential. There is nothing wrong with you as a parent for having a period of disconnection with your child, and it's not your fault. It is probably a reflection of the ways you have been struggling or hurt in the present or in your own childhood.

Be open with your feelings

You can talk about what's happened and why the connection seems broken. You can also talk in general about whatever your mind wanders to. You can express some of the grief you may feel, or the frustration you have with your child's behaviour. You can talk about any despair you feel and why it sometimes seems hard to repair the connection.

You can express feelings of helplessness, and the hopelessness of changing the situation. You can also see if your current situation reminds you of earlier hurts you experienced.

Listening time does often work like waving a magic wand. I usually find that any problem I talk about in listening time looks slightly different when I come back to that situation.

Sometimes, what makes a problem hard to deal with is actually partly not about the present but about the past. We might have been in a similar situation that we didn't heal from, so we are still carrying old feelings. When these have been released, we get a shift in perception. It's as if our feelings are veils over reality, and as we take away each veil, through talking, laughing and crying, the situation looks a little different.

If there is a particular area in which we are having difficulty, some focused listening time can help; for example, when I struggled to play and laugh with my daughter after my grand-mother's death, I decided to do some play-focused listening time with another partner. We each talked about how play was going for us, and it really helped.

Listening time will help clear your mind and make you feel better. Things will probably improve immediately to some extent, because your child senses that you feel better and so will start to feel better too. You can think more clearly about using the Hand in Hand Parenting tools, and how to connect with your child. You might also get some good ideas about how to make your relationship stronger.

When we feel more positive about the situation ourselves, we are in a better position to help our child catch up with their own emotional healing process. We can help them to heal the hurt from whatever happened. It might be challenging, because they have a backlog of feelings, but by giving ourselves extra support we are in a better position to do the extra work.

Spending time together with your child

The next step is to do something fun with your child. When we are dealing with major life events or challenging behaviour, life can get pretty serious. If we've been struggling with their feelings and our own, we are most likely not experiencing the joy of parenting.

It might be that you start with something that you know you will enjoy too, which is easy and relaxing for both of you: perhaps going swimming or to the cinema, or a theme park or having an ice cream.

This can be like a warm-up to the next step, which is to plan a long special time for your child – perhaps 24 or 48 hours, where you can be alone together to re-bond. Tell your child that it will be special time, and that they can do whatever they want for this time period. If they are old enough, you can talk together and plan what to do in advance. It's really important that this time is completely one-to-one time without anyone else around, so it might take some organisation to make it work. Perhaps you could go away together for a weekend somewhere of their choice, or just hang out at home if possible.

During this long special time, it's especially important to remember to say yes to whatever your child asks for, providing it's not dangerous or harmful to others. Saying yes is a brilliant strategy, because it immediately takes away the conflict that we can sometimes get caught in when we say no. Our child feels happy because they are enjoying themselves, doing or having what they want together with us.

We've already covered the importance of saying no when our child is off-track and they need a limit. But when we have a bigger disconnection with our child they may not feel the closeness they need to release their feelings. If we set limits, we might find that they don't release any emotions, and the off-track behaviour and sense of disconnection continues.

When we say yes, we can simply hang out doing things our child loves and having fun together. We warm up their sense of connection so that they begin to feel us really present with them.

Love Bombing – far from permissive parenting

The psychologist Oliver James coined the term 'Love Bombing' for this kind of extended special time. In his book of the same name, he suggests that whenever we have a broken connection or behavioural issue with our child, we should give them a big dose of Love Bombing.

Love Bombing might seem like complete permissive parenting and the recipe for bringing up a spoilt child, but there's actually a big difference. The stereotypical view of a spoilt child is one who gets whatever they want and has a big strop whenever they don't. A spoilt child might be extremely self-absorbed and doesn't seem to care about others' feelings or needs. This stereotypical spoilt child might be rich in material possessions and getting their own way, but they are poor in emotional health and deep human connection. When they get grumpy or whiny, or only seem to think about themselves, it's actually a sign that they are full of hurt feelings. Perhaps their parent is trying to please them and make them happy, and is trying to avoid their emotional upsets by giving them everything they want. A parent might be afraid to say no because they fear the enormous meltdown that might occur. A child may then use crying as a means to try to get what they want by fake crying. A spoilt child who asks for lots of things really just wants to be happy. Beneath all the want is a need for connection and healing.

When we give our child an extended special time, we do what they want so that we are giving them some control and power. But we also give them what they really need. We hang out with them, we talk to them, we give them lots of close connection, we laugh and play with them.

The other big difference is that when the extended special time is over and we return to everyday life, we are not afraid to say no to our child, and the feelings that might come. We help our child release the feelings that get in the way of their loving, cooperative nature.

More time might mean more feelings to express

During the extended special time, our child absorbs all of our warm attention so that he senses that we are there to listen to him. The end of special time might trigger some big feelings, because he has had a much bigger dose of connection with us than he has recently had. All the upset surrounding that broken connection might come up to the surface.

Our child might be upset about special time finishing, or may be acting off-track, and we then need to set a limit. It may not come immediately. But it's quite likely that there will be a big upset simmering, which is all part of the healing process.

Hopefully, this big change, increasing our listening time and giving our child a big dose of special time, can start a new beginning for ourselves and our child.

After we start the work of rebuilding the connection with our child, we might notice that he has a lot of big upsets. He may start sensing that we are now available to listen to him and he may make up for the time when we weren't so available. This can be challenging for us, so it's really important to make sure we do enough listening time so that we are able to cope with the amount of feelings he releases. We should notice when we're feeling drained and finding it hard to cope. We should continue to do as much listening time as we need. We should also remember just to do nice things with our child so that we can simply be together and we can return to the joy of being deeply connected with our child.

Case Study: Dawn

'There was a time when I began to get really disconnected from my son. He learnt some swear words when he was in the park and he started swearing a lot. He seemed to know that it would really push my buttons and get my attention! He would also hit me a lot, and it was really hard for me to set limits in a gentle way around it.

'It got really bad to the point that if my daughters were around I would always choose to spend time with them and not him. I was really frustrated with his behaviour, and if I tried to set limits it never worked, as he would just ignore me. He didn't seem well connected enough to be able to release any feelings.

'In listening times I would realise that he reminded me of my father and brother who had hurt me physically when I was a girl. I did a lot of listening time to deal with some of the grief and fear that got triggered in me. I also talked about how much I hated the swearing.

'At some point I realised that I had to make him laugh. So I let him swear and then would try to act playful about it. I would tell him, "Don't come near me with those terrible words" and I would run away from him. He would chase me, laughing and swearing. We did this every day for a while, and it helped a lot to get the words out of his system. It was much better for him to say them just to me as part of a playful game rather than embarrass me in front of my friends!

'I wanted to warm up the connection some more, so for one month we did lots of special time, and I set very few limits. Then we had a long weekend special time where we spent two days at the beach. When we got home, I started setting more limits, and he was now able to release more feelings with me. We got more connected again, and have been much better connected ever since. We have our difficult spots, but it's never been as bad as it was. Having lots of listening time to release my deep feelings about the past really helped to get our relationship back on track.'

EXERCISE: Reflection – look at broken connections

1 If you have a sense of a broken connection with your child, when did it begin? Describe in detail how it started, and what has happened.

2 Does the broken connection remind you of anything that happened in your own childhood?

3 How would you like things to be in your family? Create a verbal picture of your perfect family life, or write it down.

CHAPTER 18

Conclusion: Imagine a Society of Listeners

•

'Crying is one of the highest devotional songs.
One who knows crying, knows spiritual practice.
If you can cry with a pure heart, nothing else
compares to such a prayer. Crying includes
all the principles of Yoga.'

Kripalvanandji

Following the steps outlined in this book can transform your parenting and your life. You can help your child to heal and recover from any stress and upset they experience so that they don't have to carry heavy baggage into adulthood. Behaviour issues improve when we give our children the quality attention they need to process their feelings. Parenting becomes easier and much more joyful.

This knowledge of the healing power of tears allows us to connect with our children on a deeper level than we may have ever imagined possible. When our children get upset, we don't need to withdraw our attention. Instead, we can meet our child exactly where they are with the listening they need to heal.

When they act off-track, we don't need to withdraw our attention in an attempt to give a punishment or find a consequence for their actions. We can simply be there and find a way to connect with them when they need us most. Through play, laughter and listening to upsets, we can help them to heal the hurt that caused their behaviour.

We can cry ourselves

When I was younger, I often wondered why so many of the people I knew had fragmented and distanced relationships with their parents. Perhaps it's because our own parents weren't well emotionally resourced and couldn't listen to our feelings or understand the importance of doing so. We often had to deal with our feelings alone, which can create a rift between ourselves and our parents. We sometimes find relationships difficult in general because we carry so much hurt from the past.

When parenting becomes hard, we can use listening time to process the emotions that get triggered, and in doing so our children can be our greatest teachers, finding the parts of ourselves where we still carry hurt. We can experience the healing benefits of crying ourselves. We can return to our children able to give them the attention they need and follow our natural instinct to be there for them unconditionally, no matter what emotions they are expressing or how they are behaving.

Closeness that lasts

Being there whenever our child needs us has a powerful effect on our relationship with them. It means that even as they grow older, into the teenage years and adulthood, we retain a close connection with them. Because we didn't withdraw our attention when they were hurt or behaved challengingly, they will feel accepted by us without judgement. They will feel safe to come to us with their emotions, trusting that we will listen and understand.

In the UK one in four adults have a mental health problem at some point in their life. What if the healing power of tears is the missing piece of information that we need to reduce this statistic?

Having a close connection to our teenagers has been shown by research to be a super-protective factor that prevents adverse adolescent outcomes such as teenage pregnancy, violence or drug addiction. When we help our children with the feelings that get in the way of being closely connected we give them the security they need to thrive.

Having an outlet to heal our stress and upset means that we can get on with living our lives to the full, without emotional difficulties getting in the way of our close connections with family and friends. We can heal our feelings so that our relationships with others can become easier and closer.

We no longer need to be alone with our feelings. We can receive unconditional empathy from connecting with other like-minded parents who understand that we are always doing our best, who understand that when we have struggles it's because our own childhood story makes the present difficult and that it's not our fault.

A new way of listening for the new generation

We are really the first generation of parents who are starting to listen. We are just beginning to understand what it means to heal ourselves, as well as helping our children to heal too. This emotional work isn't easy, and our journey won't be perfect. But the reward is that we get to experience a deep connection with our children, and they can grow up with a deep sense of well-being, being able to live joyful, fulfilling lives.

Have you ever read a book that promised to change your life, and while you read it it seemed amazing? Then, afterwards, perhaps you incorporated some of the book's suggestions into your life, but forgot other parts, until reading the book was just a distant memory? I hope that you'll find that reading this book is about more than just words on paper. There is a way that you can keep this book alive for the rest of your life and that is to connect with other parents. Our human minds work best in a system. When we think and connect with other people, we are inspired, we encourage each other and we can continue to build on what we have learnt. I hope you'll discover other Hand in Hand Parenting parents in your area through courses or social networking. Together we can build communities of parents listening to children.

I can remember the relief of starting my own Hand in Hand Parenting group, and how it felt, when my daughter started to cry, I knew that I wouldn't be judged or expected to make her stop as quickly as possible. In that safe space it was understood and accepted that my job as a parent was to listen.

Take a course or find a listening partner. Tell your partner or friend all about this book. Together we can build a different kind of society, one of listening. We can extend this empathy outwards to other parents and other children that we meet. We can live without judgement, just an understanding of the feelings and stories that make up the rich tapestry of our lives.

We can stop and feel the grief and hurt that we have been carrying through all these years. We can find a deeper happiness. Then we can do the same for our children. Tears are the way.

About Hand in Hand Parenting

Hand in Hand Parenting is a non-profit organisation founded by Patty Wipfler in 1989. The organisation offers free articles and teleseminars, and, for a fee, online and in-person classes and consultations. Instructors are active in many countries. Visit www.handinhandparenting.org for more information and to find your nearest instructor.

Further Reading

For more about the brain science in this book, I can recommend these books by Dr Daniel Siegel:

Parenting from the Inside Out, Dr Daniel J. Siegel and Dr Mary Hartzell, Penguin 2004
The Whole-Brain Child, Dr Daniel J. Siegal and Tina Payne Bryson, Robinson, 2012

The following books are congruent with the Hand in Hand Parenting approach:

Listen: Five Simple Tools to Meet Your Everyday Parenting Challenges, Hand in Hand Parenting, Patty Wipfler and Tosha Schore M.A., 2016
The Art Of Roughhousing, Good Old Fashioned Horseplay and Why Every Kid Needs It, Dr Anthony Benedet and Lawrence J. Cohen PhD, Quirk Books, 2011 (tips for fun physical play with our children)
The Opposite Of Worry, Lawrence J. Cohen PhD, Balantine Books, 2013 (ideas to help children with fears and anxiety based on a playful, listening approach)
Playful Parenting, Lawrence J. Cohen PhD, Balantine Books, 2012 (lots of games and ideas that are very similar to playlistening)

The following books are about Aletha Solter's 'Aware Parenting' approach, which is similar to Hand in Hand Parenting:

Attachment Play, Aletha Solter PhD, Shining Star Press, 2014
The Aware Baby, Aletha Solter PhD, Shining Star Publications, 2001
Helping Young Children Flourish, Aletha Solter PhD, Shining Star Press, 1989

References

Introduction

1 Dr W.H. Frey and M. Langseth, *Crying – The Mystery of Tears*, Winston Press, 1985
2 Osho, *Emotional Wellness: Transforming Fear, Anger, and Jealousy into Creative Energy*, Harmony, 2007
3 Aletha Solter, *The Aware Baby*, Shining Star Publications, 2001
4 Aletha Solter, *The Aware Baby*
5 www.handinhandparenting.org, includes articles and resources by Patty Wipfler and other Hand in Hand Parenting instructors
6 http://www.handinhandparenting.org/2011/12/holding-a-limit-can-make-bathtime-much-more-fun/

Chapter 1

1 Dr Daniel Siegel and Dr Mary Hartzell discuss this research in detail in *Parenting From the Inside Out*, Penguin, 2004
2 Aletha Solter, *The Aware Baby*, Shining Star Publications, 2001
3 Louise DeSalvo, *Writing as a Way of Healing: How Telling Our Stories Transforms Our Lives*, Beacon Press, 2001
4 P. Rautava, L. Lehtonen and H. Helenius, 'Infantile colic: Child and family three years later', *Pediatrics*, 1995, edition 96
5 You can read more about the development of the brain in *The Whole-Brain Child*, by Dr Daniel Siegel and Tina Payne Bryson, Robinson, 2012

Chapter 2

1 You can read more about this in *Parenting From the Inside Out*, by Dr Daniel Siegel and Dr Mary Hartzell, Penguin, 2004
2 Wendy Middlemiss, Douglas A. Granger, Wendy A. Goldberg and Laura Nathans, 'Asynchrony of mother–infant hypothalamic–pituitary–adrenal axis activity following extinction of infant crying responses induced during the transition to sleep', *Early Human Development*, 2011
3 Thomas Lewis, Fari Amini and Richard Lannon, *A General Theory of Love*, Vintage, 2001
4 You can read more about this in Daniel J. Siegel and Mary Hartzell, *Parenting From the Inside Out*

Chapter 3

1 Daniel J. Siegel and Mary Hartzell, *Parenting From the Inside Out*, Penguin, 2004
2 Patty Wipfler, *Listening to Children*, Hand in Hand Parenting, 2006
3 Anthony Benedet and Lawrence J. Cohen, *The Art of Roughhousing, Good Old Fashioned Horseplay and Why Every Kid Needs It*, Quirk Books, 2011 (tips for fun physical play with our children)

Chapter 4

1 Thomas Lewis, Fari Amini and Richard Lannon, *A General Theory of Love*, Vintage, 2001

Chapter 5

1 Patty Wipfler, *Healing Children's Fears*, from the *Listening to Children Booklets*, Hand in Hand Parenting, 2006
2 Bruce Alexander, 'Rat Park', *British Columbia Journal*, 1980; Bruce Alexander, *The Globilisation of Addiction*, Oxford University Press, 2010

Chapter 6

1   Aletha Solter, *Tears and Tantrums*, Shining Star Press, 1998
2   You can read more about brain development in *The Whole Brain-Child*, Daniel J. Siegel and Tina Payne Bryson, Robinson, 2012
3   Dr Daniel Siegel and Dr Mary Hartzell, *Parenting From the Inside Out*, Penguin, 2004

Chapter 7

1   You can read more about this in Patty Wipfler, *Listening to Children*, Hand in Hand Parenting, 2006

Chapter 8

1   Thomas R. Verny, *The Secret Life of the Unborn Child*, Summit Books, 1981
2   P. Rautava, L. Lehtonen and H. Helenius, 'Infantile colic: Child and family three years later', *Pediatrics*, 1995, edition 96
3   You can read more about this in *The Aware Baby*, by Aletha Solter, Shining Star Publications, 2001
4   See 'Must Parents be Consistent?' by Patty Wipfler, http://www.handinhandparenting.org/article/must-parents-consistent/

Chapter 10

1   Patty Wipfler coined this term in Hand in Hand's 'Parenting by Connection Starter Class' course materials

Chapter 11

1   You can read more about this in Anthony Benedet and Lawrence J. Cohen, *The Art of Roughhousing: Good Old Fashioned Horseplay and Why Every Kid Needs it*, Quirk Books, 2011
2   Madan Kataria, *Laugh for No Reason*, Madhuri International, 1999

Chapter 13

1   You can read more about this in *The Aware Baby*, by Aletha Solter, Shining Star Publications, 2001
2   https://www.psychologytodaycom/blog/sleeping-angels/201205why-laughing-in-the-evening-helps-you-sleep-better-night
3   William Sears, *A Parents Guide To Understanding and Preventing Sudden Infant Death Syndrome*, Little, Brown, 1996
4   See the Infant Sleep Information Service for more information about safe sleeping for infants, https://www.isisonline.org.uk
5   P. Mooney, C.A. Espie and N.M. Broomfield, 'An experimental assessment of a Pennebaker writing intervention in primary insomnia', in *Behavioral Sleep Medicine*, Vol. 7, Issue 2, 2009

Index